THE MORBID CURIOUS

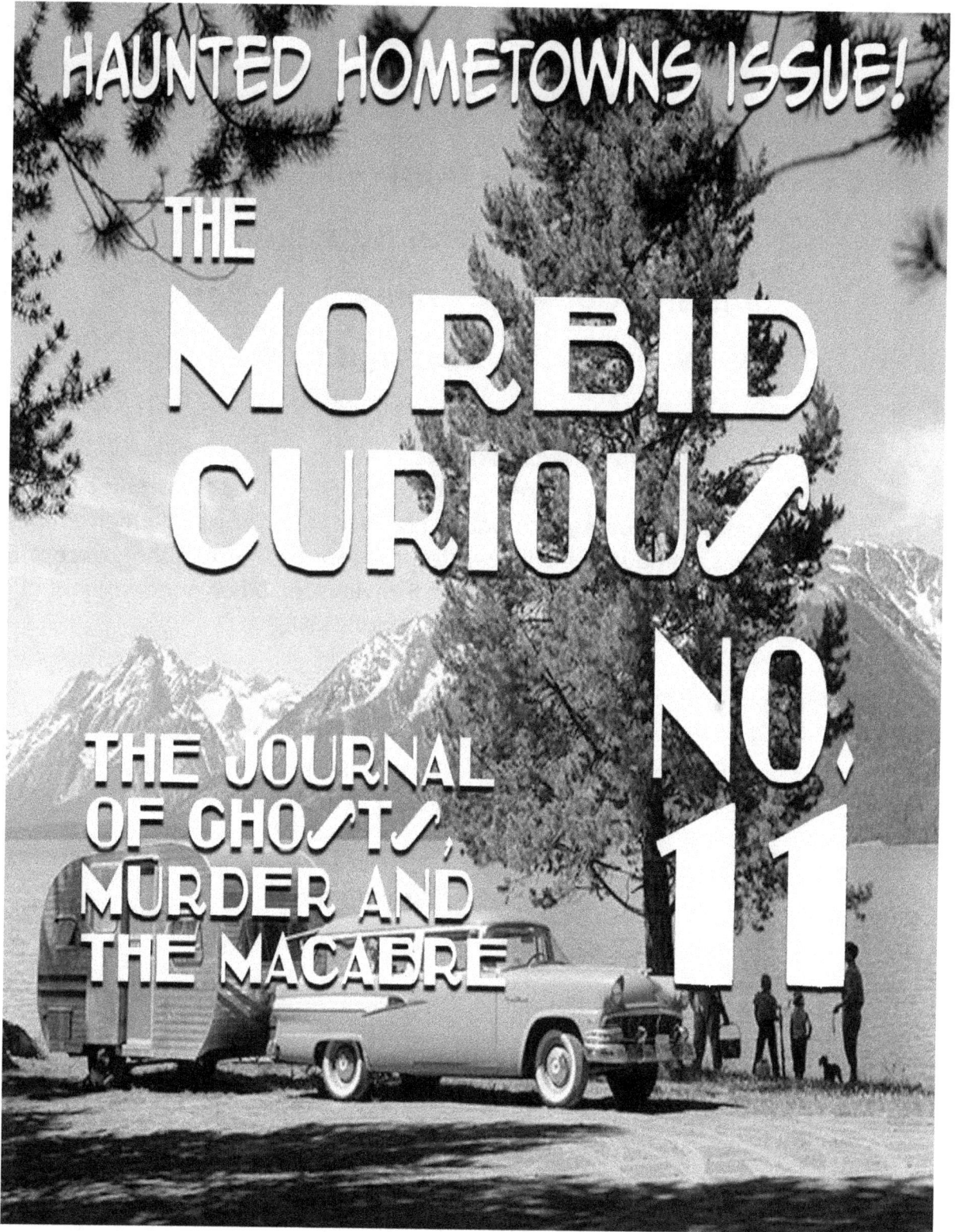

HAUNTED HOMETOWNS ISSUE!

THE

MORBID CURIOUS

THE JOURNAL OF GHOSTS, MURDER AND THE MACABRE

NO. 11

MORBID CURIOUS NO. 11

Published by American Hauntings Ink

301 East Broadway – Alton, IL – 62oo2

www.americanhauntingsink.com

Cover Design by April Slaughter

Editor and Interior Design by Troy Taylor

Contact: ghosts@americanhauntings.net

First Edition – April 2025

Printed in the United States of America

ISBN: 978-1-958589-22-9

TABLE OF CONTENTS

UNREQUITED LOVE AT MURDER CREEK

AMANDA R. WOOMER

WESTERN NEW YORK IS FILLED WITH LEGENDS AND LORE. WITH A RICH INDIGENOUS HISTORY COUPLED WITH BATTLES FROM THE FRENCH AND INDIAN WAR, THE AMERICAN REVOLUTION, AND THE WAR OF 1812, STORIES OF TRAGEDY, DEATH, AND GHOSTS ARE BOUND TO APPEAR IN THE DARKER ANNALS OF OUR LOCAL HISTORY.

And while Murder Creek in Akron, New York, may have gotten its macabre name from a story surrounding two ill-fated lovers—Ah-weh-hah and Tah-yoh-ne—and their conflict with a white man named Sanders, another murder took place 70 years later that solidified the legend of Murder Creek into Western New York legend.

The case of Sarah Ann "Sadie" McMullen baffled doctors and officials when the trial gripped Buffalo media in 1891. What initially appeared as a case of a young woman's affections going unrequited devolved into the misogynistic study of what mania, melancholia, and one's menstrual cycle could lead a teenage girl to do.

Sadie McMullen was born in Chicago, Illinois, on January 6, 1873, to Mary Cunningham and William F. McMullen. Born three years after her parents were married, her older brother died in infancy, and her younger sister Josephine was born two years later. Her father was described as an alcoholic and "stern and austere" and was said to make life for his family "one of misery, poverty, and wretchedness." Her mother was said to be an "irritable, quick-tempered, troublesome woman with suicidal and homicidal tendencies." While such origins could help build a case against Sadie's family history, doctors went even further into her familial background. They discovered that her grandparents were first cousins, alcoholism ran rampant through multiple generations, her grandfather suffered from delusions and paranoia, and several aunts and uncles were locked in insane asylums, with one described as "light in the head" and another diagnosed with dementia.

The Buffalo State Hospital is now known as the Richardson-Olmstead Complex and towers over the Elmwood Village in Buffalo.

Numerous family members were living in either the Buffalo State Hospital or the insane department at the Erie County Almshouse. To the doctors searching for a root cause of Sadie's psychosis, her family history was damning.

When Sadie was just two years old, she was fast asleep on the family couch when her father watched her sit up and start crying and laughing. After a moment, she fell back onto her pillow, where she began frothing at the mouth, and her arms and legs lashed out wildly. Sadie was promptly diagnosed with epilepsy and started the appropriate treatment that seemed to help significantly.

In 1876, on Halloween night (a date that would become a tragic one for Sadie McMullen), it's said Mary Cunningham McMullen died at just 23 years old from shock after being chased by a bear. Around this time, Sadie would also begin to enter trances where she would lose consciousness and wander into the woods for hours.

By the time Sadie was 11 years old, her father decided, after living in Illinois, Wisconsin, and Missouri, that he wanted to see the East. In the spring of 1884, he and his children began the long journey as they walked from Missouri to New York. While traveling to New York, Sadie continued to experience moments of lost consciousness and move about unknowingly—she would sometimes wake up to find herself picking berries in the woods or soaking wet. Once settled in Akron, New York (approximately 30 miles northeast of Buffalo) in the fall of 1884, Sadie was now required to run the household herself while still struggling with her bouts of unconsciousness. The family fell into a routine of little consequence until Sadie befriended the Brown brothers at 16.

While Sadie and the younger Brown brother were close, she also became acquainted with the young man's older brother, Simon Brown, a married man with a little girl named Delia. Shortly after befriending the Browns, Simon's wife died, and Simon hired Sadie to help run his house and help with his daughter, who was now six years old. According to friends and family, Sadie took her role seriously in the Brown household and was said to shower Delia with maternal love.

The following year, Sadie was brought to Buffalo, where she lived with her aunt and worked as a housekeeper on Delaware Avenue. While living with her aunt, the older woman described Sadie as "cowardly, superstitious, easily frightened, and a firm believer in dreams and in ghosts."

Despite Sadie's unusual behavior and continued epileptoid episodes, she managed to maintain a relatively normal life, spending her time traveling between Buffalo and Akron. But all that changed in October 1890 when tragedy struck at the hands of Sadie McMullen.

Sadie returned to Akron for a church festival on October 25, 1890, and stayed with the Brown family. During Sadie's visit, the Browns saw it as an excuse to celebrate. On Halloween, they invited the daughter of a family friend–Nellie May Connor–over to spend the day with Sadie, Delia, and Delia's Aunt Hannah. The girls sang songs, danced, and played games, but when Sadie received a letter from her former employer in Buffalo accusing her of stealing diamonds, Sadie's demeanor changed. Undoubtedly upset by the accusation, Sadie began to spiral downward and decided to write a suicide note to her aunt.

A stone bridge over Murder Creek as seen from Akron Falls Trail.

Photo courtesy of Andre Carrotflower

While a suicide note seemed like a dramatic response to a petty accusation from a former employer (one that ended up being disproven), it looks as if other things had been eating away at Sadie over the last few years. She wrote that she was "sik [sic] and tired of living," and that "when I am dead, I will come to you and explain." As Sadie continued to write, she revealed what was torturing her: she was in love with Simon Brown. She admits in the letter that she leaves her heart in Akron despite her feelings going unrequited and that after she is dead, "the man I love will know me as a frequent visitor." She requested to be buried in Akron, not to be near her father and sister but "near my loved one." Perhaps the most chilling part of the letter was when Sadie admitted, "I think I will take someone with me."

Still upset, Sadie told Aunt Hannah that she intended to visit her friend in Falkirk (a suburb of Akron). Not wanting to miss out on any time with Sadie, Delia asked if she could go but Aunt Hannah only agreed if Nellie May went too, setting the tragedy in motion.

The three girls set off with Sadie stopping at the post office to send her letter and the grocery store. Sadie walked hand in hand with Delia and Nellie May, as witnessed by the grocer and a group of boys playing nearby.

The trio reached a trestle bridge that ran 35 feet high. Once on the bridge, Sadie sat on the edge, kicking her feet back and forth as she leaned over and looked down at the water below.

Without warning, Sadie leaped up, grabbed Nellie May, and, after a short struggle with the 10-year-old, pushed the girl off the bridge. Turning on Delia, Sadie placed a hand over the girl's mouth before throwing her from the bridge, too. However, instead of killing herself at that moment, as her suicide note stated, Sadie wandered off the bridge and went to visit her priest and told him goodbye. She then returned to Simon Brown's house where she bade Aunt Hannah goodbye before running from the house.

A short while passed before a young boy came running into the Browns' house, saying he saw Sadie jump off the bridge into Murder Creek. Without hesitating, Simon Brown ran from the home to the creek, pulling her out of the water. She kicked and screamed as she struggled to get back to the water, shouting, "Oh! Let me back! Oh! Let me back!"

Once back at the Brown house, Simon laid her on the couch, where the doctor was able to check the young woman. He determined that she had experienced an epileptic seizure, which had led to her falling into the creek. As Sadie continued to come to, Simon Brown and Aunt Hannah finally asked where the children were. Sadie's chilling response: "What children?"

Unsure why her clothes and hair were wet, Sadie seemed to have no memory of how she ended up in the creek, much less what had happened to the two little girls

Sketch of Sadie McMullen at her trial from The *Evening World*, March 7, 1891.

who had left the house with her hours before.

The community began searching for Delia Brown and Nellie May Connor and finally found them shortly before dawn the next day in the ravine under the trestle bridge. Nellie May was found dead, "cruelly bruised, and her brains had been dashed out." Shockingly, the six-year-old Delia was still alive and "lingered between life and death for several weeks before recovering." Nellie May was buried in St. Teresa's Roman Catholic Cemetery, and Sadie was brought to the Erie County Jail the next day.

In the days following the Halloween tragedy at Murder Creek, doctors observed Sadie. Despite what she had done to Delia and Nellie May, the doctors saw Sadie as a "frail, delicate young woman." Initially, it seemed as if Sadie was incapable of such a crime, but as doctors continued to study her throughout the fall and winter, they also noticed her "dull and apathetic eyes" and her "black and feelingless expression." When questioned about Halloween night, Sadie claimed she remembered receiving the letter accusing her of theft and then feeling her wet hair on the couch. She also insisted she couldn't believe Nellie was dead, much

SADIE M'MULLEN IS INSANE.

The Akron Child Murderess to Go to an Asylum.

less understand how she could have done it.

Sadie's trial before the court of Oyer and Terminer ("to hear and to determine"–the same system used in the Salem Witch Trials) began on March 5, 1891, and lasted only three days. The defense claimed that Sadie was in an epileptoid state made even more powerful by her menstrual cycle and therefore not responsible for her actions at that time—seemingly unconscious from when she left the post office at 5:00pm until she was laid on the couch at 9:00pm. However, prosecutors insisted that Sadie's letter sent to her aunt shortly before the tragedy was enough evidence to prove that this was a premeditated act. Sadie insisted she had never seen the letter and that it was a forgery.

Sadie McMullen was tried for first-degree murder, and if found guilty, she would be the first woman in New York State to be executed in the electric chair. As the charges were being read, it is said Sadie, "who had been as stoical when she came in as she had been during her confinement in prison, grew pale, flushed painfully, and then went all to pieces." Sadie entered a plea of insanity, and after just 30 minutes, the jury returned with a verdict. When they declared not guilty, she "screamed hysterically." Judge Lewis committed her to the Buffalo State Hospital and ordered her to stay there until she was "cured."

Sadie would spend the next three years in the Buffalo State Hospital (today known as the Richardson-Olmstead Complex) before being released in August 1893. Some stories claim that she married E.A. Hays–her defense lawyer. However, Sadie McMullen seems to have vanished from records, with some people believing she moved from New York and made her way across the country to California.

Murder Creek has a way of haunting the town of Akron, from the star-crossed lovers Ah-weh-hah and Tah-yoh-ne (whose spirits are said to actually haunt the waters) to the disturbing murder and attempted suicide of Sadie McMullen. Whether the death of Nellie May Connor was at the hands of a bitter young woman scorned by unrequited love, or an accident hidden in the shadows of a trance will only continue to add to the mystery and tragedy of Murder Creek.

THE AXMAN COMETH TO COLORADO SPRINGS

ERIN TAYLOR

ON THE MORNING OF JUNE 8, 1912, IN VILLISCA, IOWA, EIGHT BODIES WERE FOUND BLUDGEONED TO DEATH IN A FARMHOUSE AT THE EDGE OF TOWN. BUT BEFORE THAT DARK NIGHT, ANOTHER TERRIBLE CRIME WAS COMMITTED IN COLORADO SPRINGS. THE CULPRIT WAS NEVER CAUGHT NOR IDENTIFIED, A MYSTERY TO THIS VERY DAY.

On the morning of June 8, 1912, in Villisca, Iowa, eight bodies were found bludgeoned in a farmhouse. Mr. and Mrs. Joseph Moore, their four children, and two neighboring children were tucked in their beds when the killer took his swing on each. The heads were draped with bed clothing, while the windows were covered with skirts and aprons. Just as quietly as he snuck in, he slipped out into the night. The assailant used the family's ax, leaving it bloodied on the property. Blade marks were gouged into the slanted ceiling where the weapon struck as it swung. There was and still is speculation that the killer hid in the attic before his deadly spree, just through a small doorway across from the parent's bed at the top of the stairs. The town was in an uproar; accusations flew- the news of the dead was sensationalized, so much so that it wiped the April 1912 sinking of the Titanic off the front page. The house and its story are infamous within paranormal lore; television shows and books have researched the location extensively. The murders remain unsolved to this day.

But there's so much more.

Before that night at Villisca, a terrible crime was committed against two families in Colorado Springs, nestled in the foothills of the Rocky Mountains. The Burnham and Wayne families were discovered dead in their beds... butchered, their houses right beside each other. The culprit was never caught nor identified, a mystery to this very day.

In September of 1911, Nettie Ruth stopped by the 321 West Dale Street house to visit with her sister, Alice "May" Burnham. There was no answer at the door, and she was concerned as the windows were dark. A neighbor had a key to the house, but the door wouldn't budge. After using force to gain entry, she entered the home to an overwhelming smell of decay. Bedclothes darkened the house by covering the windows. In the bedroom, she found her sister and the children, Nellie Emma (6) and John "Johnny" Jr. (3), dead on a single bed;

The Arthur Burnham Family

their heads appeared to have been split. One of the children may have tried to run, based on how their body fell against the bed. The killer had taken great care to cover the bodies with mundane clothes, which soaked up the blood. One of these items happened to be the girl's small jacket.

A pet parrot sat aloof nearby, reportedly unfazed by the gruesome scene.

A similar scene played out next door at 743 Harrison Place. Henry Wayne (30), his wife, Blanche (26), and their daughter (1 or 2) were all found deceased in bed. Somehow, in the course of the night, six people were slaughtered between the two houses, all fatal blows to the head. Interestingly, the families were friends, as the Waynes had just moved to the area from Indiana three weeks prior.

The Modern Woodmen Sanitarium where Arthur Burnham was being treated for tuberculosis at the time of the murders.

Within hours, members of the morbidly curious lined the streets with their vehicles, craning their necks to glimpse the terrible scene. The bloody weapon was quickly discovered nearby; a neighbor, Mrs. Evans, confirmed that she had recently lent the ax to Mr. Burnham.

Arthur J. Burnham, the husband of the deceased woman of the Burnham home, was not there, which made him the immediate suspect. Battling consumption (tuberculosis), he was working and living nine miles away at the Modern Woodmen Sanitarium. "I didn't do this," he exclaimed, expressing that his wife must have an enemy. Mr. Burnham was significantly physically weak from the illness, and it was speculated that there was no way he could have walked the distance to murder his family to turn around and retrace his steps. Police still detained Mr. Burnham and dragged him to see the bloody scene, including the bodies. It was likely to be a

way to elicit guilty admission from him. In an interesting twist, he asked to see the bodies of his children but not his wife. Despite having a strong alibi with the sanitarium, police kept him in custody, concerned that the man appeared to have no emotional response to the deaths of his family. Perhaps it was shock?

"Don't waste your time with me," he pled to the police.

The deceased Wayne family was sent back to Indiana for burial, while the Burnhams were buried in the local Evergreen Cemetery. Sadly, Arthur Burnham died from complications from tuberculosis, asthma, and kidney disease in February 1912. He was interred alongside his family.

Two underage ladies from the streets asserted that they knew who was responsible for the horrific acts. They wove a tale about a gambling den where Mr. Wayne won a considerable amount, which irritated some other gamblers. The story alleged that a mystery man, only known by his first name, Harry, and his Italian friend, Donatel (or Donatello), demanded Wayne give back the money or lose his life. According to one of the girls, Mrs. Burnham had overheard this and threatened to call the police. After the killings, the girls heard an admission, "Yes,

(Left) the Burnham house after the murders and (Right) The Wayne House

we murdered them," before Harry supposedly got on a train with a clean, shaven face and derby hat, never to be seen again. And Donatel? He was found, questioned, and very confused as he was unaware of any such person. One rumor speculated that the Italian was interested in the older Alice Burnham and was jealous, which might have led him to kill. He was never formally charged for the murders.

What if the Waynes were murdered by accident? The neighboring cottages were said to be almost identical. Another tale spouted that the Wayne family was not the intended hit; the killer entered their home by mistake, possibly confusing the houses. Then, he had to fix his error by entering the planned initial house for an unintended double feature.

Perhaps a deranged person broke into the house? An inkwell was tipped over, and smudged fingerprints were found where the killer must have made a mess on the wash bin. Mercury was used to capture the perfect print on the ax handle. In both houses, lamps were moved, and strangely, the flue had been removed (James & James, 2017). There was no imminent sign of a robbery, and jewelry was left nearby within the site. The assailant might have tried to hide his work by burning down the Burnham's house- a charred lining of curtain and burnt piece of newspaper was discovered on the floor. There was a later account in which a newspaper reporter claimed that flash powder ignited the small blaze. Bill James, author of the 2017 book *The Man From The Train*, disagreed with the reporter's statement and remarked that the potential serial killer would later set fire to other houses. The newspaper was the perfect kindling.

On the west side of the state, a man by the name of George Casey turned himself in to Ouray police later in the month, declaring he was responsible for the murders in Colorado Springs. Escorted to the city, it soon became pretty clear that he had nothing to do with the acts- he had been locked up in a Montrose County jail during the times of the suspected deaths on an "account of lunacy."

The idea of a maniac on the loose was short-lived, but there would be other theories. The houses on Dale and Harrison were also close to the train tracks. The train makes travel easy if you need to escape out of town or out of state quickly. The following month in Monmouth, Illinois, another family was bludgeoned by an ax- police found a flashlight that was inscribed with the words "Colorado Springs September 4". Two weeks later, a family in Ellsworth, Kansas, was also slaughtered. The motive seemed similar: not a robbery, all families, and the killer gained access through open windows. Low lighting from a candle was said to have been used so as not to wake his victims. These houses were also near the tracks. The winter was calm before three families were found in the same devastating outcomes in Paola, Kansas, Villisca, Iowa, and Blue Island, Illinois.

Police investigated several suspects across the states, but no one was found guilty of the heinous acts. Fingerprints from the various scenes were analyzed, compared, and thrown out. There were other murders that some argued may have been committed by the same person, as the ax was a weapon of easy access. However, these few Midwest crimes all had striking similarities. The killer covered the bodies and the windows and kept the light low. Who was responsible for these acts?

Whether the work of one versus many, many may not know the one tragedy that unfolded in our city. It is an unsolved crime that is still taught to new police cadets going through the academy to understand the horrors that came before them. To date, the person or persons responsible for the deaths of the Waynes and the Burnhams have not been found. A secret that was likely taken to the grave. The houses where the grisly scenes occurred on Dale Street and Harrison Place no longer stand. Today, both are vacant lots; "razing the homes on the dead-end street was the best way to rid the property of the ghosts and sweep away the unsavory memories" (Waters, 2012). Is it haunted? I cannot say for sure. Some believe so; I have no reason to doubt.

Perhaps one day, we will know the answer to who committed such atrocities. For now, in Colorado Springs, an empty lot, the history and ghost stories remain.

"GOD MUST HAVE DONE IT, NOT I!"

THE PORTWOOD MURDERS OF 1905

TROY TAYLOR

The Portwood House in Moweaqua. It was only identified as a "house in the northeast part of town" in newspapers from 2905, but growing up there, I knew exactly where it was.

EIGHTY YEARS LATER, IT WAS STILL THE MOST famous murder and suicide in the small town where I grew up. I lived on an Illinois farm during my adolescent and teenage years, and the closest town to us was a place called Moweaqua (a Native American word that was said to mean "muddy water.") It was a rural community, built up around farming and a coal mine that closed after a disaster in 1932 that killed fifty-four miners. But the Portwood Murder was still whispered about after eight decades and was still distantly recalled as one of the dark spots in the town's history.

It happened on September 10, 1905. Henry Portwood was a wealthy retired farmer who had owned a large farm about two miles east of town until 1903. He was respected and generally well-liked in the community. He had served in the Union Army during the Civil War, enlisting in 1862 at age seventeen, and was a quiet and industrious man. After he retired from farming, he purchased a home from H.C. O'Dell, which was located on the northeast edge of Moweaqua. On Sunday morning, September 10, he cut the throat of his fourth wife—nearly severing her head, the newspaper said – before slashing his own throat with a straight razor. Mrs. Portwood died quickly but her husband lived for several hours, first claiming that "God" had killed his wife and then confessing when he was told that his son would be blamed for the crime. The boy, Everett, age nine, had discovered his father and stepmother lying in pools of blood on their bedroom floor and was the first to raise the alarm about the tragic event. Ironically, it was Everett who was the source of the problems between the husband and wife, which led to the murder-suicide.

The newspapers stated, "Moweaqua is greatly excited because of the awful deed of the enraged husband."

Portwood had been a widower three times over. All his previous wives had died, including Everett's mother, who passed away in 1902. This never generated much sympathy from his fourth wife, Mollie. Just twelve years younger than her husband, Mary Helen Doyle, who went by the name of Mollie, was born in Bunker Hill, Illinois, and had moved to Moweaqua with her family when she was a child. As far as I can learn, she had never been married before becoming engaged to Portwood, who began courting her the same year that his third wife passed away. It was a troubled marriage, and Mollie never got along with Everett. She constantly complained about the boy, perhaps because he served as a reminder of Portwood's previous marriage or because of the boy's behavior, since those who knew the family stated that she was often angry because Portwood would never allow her to discipline the boy.

The constant disagreements about Everett led to the couple separating for a brief time in July 1905. They stayed apart for about two weeks and then reconciled. According to friends and witnesses, they seemed to be getting along well, even as little as an hour before the murder took place. The Portwoods had been visiting with neighbors that Sunday morning and

MR. HENRY PORTWOOD.

Henry Portwood, the wealthy farmer who snapped one day and slaughtered his wife.

(Below: Henry's fourth wife, Mollie.)

MRS. HENRY PORTWOOD.

they seemed in good spirits, the neighbors later told police.

But around 10:30 a.m., something occurred in the Portwood home that would never be revealed. Henry Portwood took the true reason for his wife's murder to the grave. A half-hour later, young Everett walked into his parents' bedroom and found them lying there, surrounded by blood. Screaming for help, the horrified child ran out of the back door and gave the alarm to the closest neighbors. Several men ran into the Portwood house and discovered the awful scene.

The newspapers stated, "The room looked like a slaughterhouse." Mollie was lying on the floor near the window. Her head had nearly been severed from her body by the brutal force of the cut. Blood was still flowing from the gaping wound, and she twitched and gurgled, still showing signs of life. The damage that had been done to her throat prevented her from speaking. With a wound to his neck almost as deep as his wife's, Portwood was

Everett Portwood — the only survivor of the slaughter that claimed the life of his father and stepmother.

lying a short distance away, almost in the doorway to the parlor. He was still alive, his feet kicking and his legs twisting as he thrashed about in his own blood. He was obviously in terrible condition, but he was in better shape than his wife.

Looking about, the men could see that a struggle had taken place in the room. Furniture was knocked over and the bed covers were twisted onto the floor. Everything in the room, from the bed to the walls, was spattered with blood. It was, the newspaper said, "a scene more terrible than can be described."

Mollie had evidently been sitting at the north window of the bedroom, dressing her hair, when she was attacked by her husband. Bloodstains showed that she rose from her chair after she was cut. After his wife had been dealt with, Portwood had then turned the razor on himself, cutting fast and deep across his own throat.

Seeing that Portwood was still alive, one of the men pressed a cloth to his throat to try and stop the bleeding. The straight razor was on the floor, just inches from Portwood's hand. It was obvious to everyone what had happened. Cyrus Mitchell, one of the first to arrive on the scene, asked him why he had killed Mollie. But Portwood's replies were nonsensical, claiming that he had not killed his wife and that he had not been hurt. Mitchell told him that his throat had been cut, as had his wife's, and that he must have done it. He replied, "Nobody cut my throat, did they? I did not do anything to my wife or myself."

Pressed to explain, Portwood insisted, "I did not do it, God must have done it, not I."

But Mitchell didn't let up. He insisted that Portwood confess to what he had done, even stating that the police might believe that it was Everett who committed the murders if Portwood died before admitting to what had happened. Apparently, this worked because the dying man made one more statement: "Yes, I did it. But it don't make any difference why. It is all right."

And those were the last words that Portwood would say about the murder. Dr. Pratt was summoned to try and save the man's life. He sewed up the wound in his neck, but his jugular had been severed and there was little he could do for him. Henry Portwood died later that afternoon – a killer and a suicide. He never explained what had caused him to snap and murder Mollie. To this day, the motivations for the crime remain a mystery.

The bodies of the Portwoods were later examined by the Shelby County coroner and then an inquest was held on Monday. The verdict was as expected: murder and suicide. Henry was buried in Hayes Cemetery, outside of Moweaqua, and Mollie was buried separately in West Cemetery. They were divided, even in death.

As for Everett, he was taken in by his sister, Mrs. Frank Clark, Portwood's daughter with his second wife, Almira, who had died in 1883. She promised to take care of him, assuring the newspapers that he would be "well raised." From there, Everett seems to vanish from history. I could find no trace of what became of the boy whose life was shattered by a single bloody event.

I HAD NO IDEA WHAT HAPPENED to Everett, but I did know what happened to the house where the murders took place. Although gone today, it was still standing when I was in high school and, in fact, remnants of the murders remained, even eight decades later.

Even back then, if a classmate or someone in the community had a ghost story or a weird incident to talk about, I was the person they came to see. It's a reputation I've managed to maintain even after all these years.

As it turned out, an acquaintance of mine had an aunt that lived in the former Portwood house, and she insisted that the place was haunted. My friend took me over to the house to hear her stories first-hand and she described knocking sounds and eerie voices that she'd been experiencing since moving in. The thing that bothered her the most, though, were the footsteps – heavy, pacing steps that sounded like a man walking around with boots on. The first few times she heard them, she was terrified, assuming someone had broken in, but she always found the house empty and the doors securely locked.

I wasn't all that surprised by the ghost stories considering what had occurred there, but I was surprised by what she showed me next. She took me down into the basement and with a flashlight, showed me the underside of the bedroom floor where Mollie and Henry had both bled to death from their wounds.

The blood had dripped between the floorboards and had stained wood on the underside. Those gruesome stains were still visible almost 80 years after their deaths.

It seemed that it wasn't just ghosts that the 1905 tragedy had left behind.

SINS OF SILENCE
THE FREEMAN MURDERS
ADAM WHITE

"DOUBLE MURDER ROCKS DECATUR: TWO YOUNG WOMEN FOUND BRUTALLY STABBED TO DEATH"

On the early morning of May 10, 1976, the city of Decatur, Illinois, was shaken to its core by a heinous double murder. The victims, two young women were found brutally stabbed to death on the city's west side, their bodies dumped like trash along West Center Street.

The investigation, led by Assistant Police Chief Horace Hoff, was swift and relentless. The police search had been meticulous, with officers scouring the area for any sign of evidence and soon Patrolman Robert Pittenger discovered items of clothing and other articles, including driver IDs belonging to the victims, in a ditch along Sunnyside Road, off old U.S. 36. Not too far from where the girls had been found.

The discovery was a crucial lead, answering one of the many questions that had been plaguing the police: who were these women? They were cousins, June Freeman, 22, was the daughter of James E. and Betty J. Brown Freeman and was employed at the Book Emporium in Northgate Mall and Marcella Sue Freeman, 23, was the daughter of Charles

T. and Lolela Brown Freeman and was employed at Osgood & Sons Inc.

As the investigation unfolded, police discovered that the women had been murdered at a location other than where their bodies were found, and that they had been transported to the dump site by a vehicle. The motive for the crime remained a mystery, but one thing was clear: the killer had acted with a level of brutality and savagery that was almost unimaginable.

The victims' families had been contacted and were left reeling, struggling to comprehend the senseless violence that had taken the lives of their loved ones, but they had to be interviewed because they might have key information about the case. While Interviewing the family, Mr. James Freeman, father of Marcella Freeman, noted that late on Sunday, May 9, the girls had gone out for Coke. It was a regular thing for the cousins to do after evening worship at the Boiling Spring Church. They would take a drive up and down Eldorado street and stop at one of the many restaurants. As the night grew later, the family knew something wasn't right because they hadn't returned home. That wasn't like them at all. It wasn't until the clock struck midnight that their concern turned to alarm and James Freeman went out to search for Marcella's car.

His quest led him to the dimly lit parking lot of McDonald's on East Eldorado Street, where he found the vehicle abandoned, its occupants

Newspaper photos pointed to where the bodies had been found on West Center Street.

nowhere to be found. With a growing sense of dread, James waited at the scene until the first light of dawn, hoping against hope that the young women would return.

But as the sun rose, the family fears only intensified, and they knew they had to involve the authorities. According to Macon County Sheriff's reports, James Freeman contacted the office at 2:44 a.m. on Monday, May 10, 1976, to report that the cousins were late arriving home. Unknown at this time, the girls had already been brutally stabbed to death on the city's west side.

On Tuesday morning, local newspapers carried pleas from the police for information that might solve the crime. Reporters also spoke with family, friends, and acquaintances of the cousins.

One of the first to be interviewed was their minister, Rev. Dewey Zinn of the Boiling Springs Church of God, located on the city's northwest side.

"These were the kind of girls who would call home if they were going to be

'We Knew Ourselves Something Was Wrong'

By Judy Tatham

Quiet and reserved, but nice. The kind of young women who didn't cause trouble — or deserve it.

These are the general characteristics acquaintances offered in describing cousins June and Marcella Freeman who met their deaths sometime after attending Sunday evening church services.

June's mother, Mrs. James Freeman, asks: "Why does something like that always happen to nice girls ... they weren't happen. They were good girls ... and I know where they are now."

city's northwest side, was expected around 7 a.m.

"They were the kind of girls who would call home if they were going to be five minutes late," Rev. Zinn says.

He described the cousins as active church members always willing to lend a hand to help with activities.

Warrensburg - Latham High School librarian Mrs. Phyllis Garbs recalls that June's acquaintances and activities seemed to be centered around the church.

"She was very quiet, but very friendly," Mrs. Garbs adds.

Marcella Freeman   June Freeman

five minutes late," Rev. Zinn recalled, his voice heavy with grief. He spoke of the cousins as active church members, always eager to lend a hand in any way they could.

At Warrensburg-Latham High School, librarian Mrs. Phillis Garbs remembered June as someone whose life revolved around the church. "She was very quiet, but very friendly," Mrs. Garbs said softly, reflecting on the girl she once knew. June had graduated in 1971, leaving behind a legacy of kindness and humility that now felt like a fading memory.

Shock and disbelief gripped her former teachers, as well as her friends from work. Mrs. Ella Cruthis, June's supervisor at the Book Emporium in Northgate Mall, was visibly shaken, tears glistening in her eyes. "I know those two kids didn't deserve what happened to them," she whispered, her voice breaking under the weight of the horror.

A co-worker, Karen Stewart, couldn't hold back her own sadness. "June was my right arm, always pitching in to help out," she said. The memory of June's warmth was painful, knowing that such a light had been so cruelly extinguished. Stewart also mentioned that the cousins were inseparable. "They were very close—like sisters," she added.

Marcella, the quieter of the two, had always kept more to herself. Mrs. Nancy Acks, dean of girls at MacArthur High School, remembered her as shy and reserved, almost a loner. Marcella had graduated in 1970, a year before her cousin, and now, those who knew her could only look back and wonder how such a tragic fate could befall two innocent souls.

June's mother, also spoke to the local paper, asking, "why does something like this always happen to nice girls? They weren't hippies, they were good girls, always have been and I know where they are now."

On May 12, a few days after the girls had been found, a cryptic tip from an anonymous informant sent shockwaves through the investigation. The informant claimed to have witnessed Michael Timothy Gibson, a 17-year-old high school student, in the company of the victims at the McDonald's where the abandoned car was discovered on the fateful night.

Police Chief Harold G. Lindsten said the boy (Michael) was arrested later on May 12 at his grandparents' home on North Gebhart, based on information received, and what followed was a chilling confession that would leave even the most seasoned investigators

The Gibson family house on Home Park Avenue.

shaken. As the truth began to unravel, a disturbing and sinister narrative emerged, revealing a sequence of events that would haunt the Freeman family and the community for years to come.

Michael stated that on the night of Sunday, May 9, a sequence of events unfolded, culminating in a heinous crime that would leave an indelible mark on the lives of all involved. It was on this evening that Gibson's path crossed with that of the Freeman women, Marcella and June, at Sandy's Drive-in. A casual acquaintance of six weeks, devoid of any romantic or intimate involvement, would soon take a dark and sinister turn.

As the trio embarked on a journey to locate another friend, their search proved fruitless, leading the girls to park their vehicle on 19th Street near the Eldorado Street McDonalds around 10 p.m.

The Freeman cousins then accompanied Gibson to his residence on Home Park Avenue. At the time, Michael's parents were out of town, caring for his 14-year-old sister, Cindy Lou Gibson, who was gravely ill and receiving treatment at the Fred Hutchinson Cancer Research Center in Seattle, Washington. Tragically, Cindy succumbed to her illness on February 23, 1977, just nine months after the murders occurred.

When they arrived, Gibson released his dogs, allowing them to roam freely, while the women explored the premises. Meanwhile, he retreated to the kitchen, where he retrieved a knife, an act he would later claim was devoid of motive or rationale.

The basement of the Home Park address became the scene of unimaginable brutality, as Gibson's invitation to the women proved to be a

25

ruse for the atrocities that were to follow. Marcella's attempt to use the bathroom was met with a vicious assault, as Gibson stabbed June multiple times, followed by a similar fate for Marcella.

June's desperate attempt to escape up the stairway was thwarted, as Gibson returned to inflict further wounds. The carnage continued, with Marcella suffering additional stab wounds, leaving behind a trail of blood and devastation.

The subsequent autopsy would reveal the true extent of the brutality, with the bodies bearing between 15 to 25 stab wounds, a grim testament to the ferocity of the attack. Gibson's confession, a haunting narrative of the events, would later reveal his callous disregard for human life, as he recounted, "There was a big mess on the floor, and I said, 'Hey, I'd better get rid of them.'" The aftermath of the crime saw Gibson dragging the lifeless bodies to his car, concealing them in the trunk, and discarding them along West Center Street Road, west of Stevens Creek, in a desperate attempt to erase the evidence of his heinous actions.

Michael Timothy Gibson, was born on May 27, 1958, in Decatur, Illinois, to Herbert E. and Jacqueline N. (Watts) Gibson. At just 17 years old, Tim was on the cusp of a milestone—graduating from MacArthur High School. He had only three weeks left until the ceremony that marked the beginning of the next chapter in his life. But that moment would never come.

Michael worked at Tolly's Market, a grocery store in the Colonial Mall, where he was a quiet yet dedicated employee. Those who knew him, whether classmates or co-workers, often described him as the type who could easily blend into the background, a bright but unassuming young man. Larry Ray, a clerk at the store, recalled how Michael's intelligence often caught people off guard.

"He's quiet but friendly," Ray said. "He knows things that most people don't—like C.B. radios. You'd start talking about them, and he'd talk your arm off."

On Monday night, just hours after the horrific discovery of the Freeman women's bodies, Ray had spoken with Michael at the store. "He didn't seem any different," Ray noted, unaware of the dark storm about to surround the boy.

Roger Burtner, the store's manager, echoed Ray's observations. He had worked closely with Michael that same evening, describing him as "clean-cut, congenial, and hardworking." Burtner remembered how Michael took pride in his work, often drawing attention to tasks he'd completed with particular care. Michael had been working at the store since August 1974, balancing his job with school as part of a work-study program. However, Burtner mentioned that Michael had recently missed some shifts to visit his younger sister, who was hospitalized in another city.

He wasn't just known as Michael to those in his life. Some called him by different names—former neighbor Wesley

Mahnken referred to him simply as "Tim," recalling the bright young boy who lived with his parents and occasionally his grandparents on North Gebhart. The MacArthur High School yearbook had yet another nickname for him: "Gibby," a nod to his involvement in the school's bands, where he had been a member for four years.

On the surface, Michael seemed like any other high school senior, quietly navigating the complexities of adolescence. But what was hiding behind that calm demeanor? And what, if anything, did it have to do with the murders of the Freeman women, discovered just hours before his shift that fateful night?

On Saturday, June 12, 1976, after being held in the Macon County Jail, Gibson of was declared mentally fit to stand trial in the Circuit Court for the murder of the two women. This ruling came after a psychiatric evaluation conducted by Dr. Dale Sunderland. Gibson's attorney, public defender Scott Diamond, had requested the examination shortly after Gibson's arrest.

"Gibson was charged with the stabbing deaths of cousins June and Marcella Freeman, whose bodies, bearing multiple stab wounds, were discovered along West Center Street Road on May 10th," the psychiatrist wrote. Dr. Sunderland submitted a three-page report to the court, in which his only publicly referenced conclusion was that Gibson understood the charges against him and could assist in his defense.

While a jury could have been convened to determine Gibson's mental fitness, neither Diamond nor State's Attorney Basil Greanias made such a request, according to Judge Scott. The trial was set for 9:30 a.m. on Thursday, June 17th, 1976, before Judge A.G. Webber III.

in Macon County Circuit Court, Judge Webber ordered that Gibson be detained on murder charges. The decision was made after Decatur police detective George McMinn testified that Gibson had twice confessed to the May 9th stabbings of June and Marcella Freeman.

McMinn's testimony followed a brief conference in chambers requested by Assistant State's Attorney Jerry Finney, who wanted the court record to show that no prejudicial questions had been asked by the state.

During the hearing, McMinn testified that Gibson had provided details about the stabbings, the crime scene, and the location of the murder weapon and some of the victims' clothing. This information was shared while McMinn and Gibson sat in a police car in Springfield on the afternoon of May 12, where Gibson had been taken for a lie detector test. According to McMinn, Gibson remarked that he was "in a bad situation" before volunteering the information.

Gibson repeated his confession after being returned to the Decatur police department, McMinn said. The confession was witnessed by another Decatur police officer.

Despite objections from Finney, citing prejudicial publicity, Webber allowed cross-examination, with Diamond asserting his right to question the witness. McMinn testified that one victim had been stabbed approximately 25 times and the other 15 times. He added that, aside from the stab wounds, the bodies were not mutilated, and there was no evidence of sexual assault.

When Judge Webber asked for the defendant's plea, public defender Scott Diamond responded, "Not guilty at this time, your honor." Gibson remained behind bars until his trial.

On August 5, 1976, after Gibson chose a non-jury trial, Judge Rodney A. Scott found him guilty of the murders, and on August 20, he was sentenced to two concurrent sentences of 35 to 65 years in prison. The defense had requested leniency, and the prosecution had asked for a 100-to-300-year sentence – the judge had compromised.

Gibson's imprisonment was marked by a series of unsuccessful parole attempts, thwarted in part by the unwavering

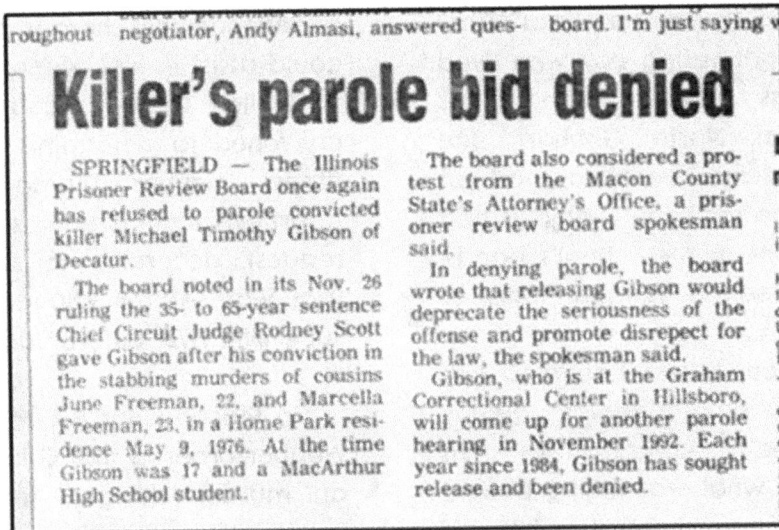

---

negotiator, Andy Almasi, answered ques- board. I'm just saying

Killer's parole bid denied

SPRINGFIELD — The Illinois Prisoner Review Board once again has refused to parole convicted killer Michael Timothy Gibson of Decatur.

The board noted in its Nov. 26 ruling the 35- to 65-year sentence Chief Circuit Judge Rodney Scott gave Gibson after his conviction in the stabbing murders of cousins June Freeman, 22, and Marcella Freeman, 23, in a Home Park residence May 9, 1976. At the time Gibson was 17 and a MacArthur High School student.

The board also considered a protest from the Macon County State's Attorney's Office, a prisoner review board spokesman said.

In denying parole, the board wrote that releasing Gibson would deprecate the seriousness of the offense and promote disrespect for the law, the spokesman said.

Gibson, who is at the Graham Correctional Center in Hillsboro, will come up for another parole hearing in November 1992. Each year since 1984, Gibson has sought release and been denied.

---

dedication of the Freeman family and their advocates.

Since 1984, the parole board had consistently rejected Gibson's requests for parole, citing the severity of the offense and the potential for his release to undermine respect for the law. In 1987, Gibson faced his third parole denial, with the board emphasizing the gravity of the crime and the necessity of safeguarding society. The Freeman family's tireless efforts to ensure justice was served played a significant role in the parole board's decisions, as they continued to advocate for Gibson's continued incarceration.

But he wouldn't stay behind bars forever.

In a shocking turn of events, Gibson was released from Graham Correctional Center in Hillsboro, Illinois, on October 8, 2002, after serving just over 26 years of his sentence. This decision was met with strong opposition from the community, particularly from the family of his victims, Marcella and June Freeman. Sergio Molina, a spokesman for the state's prisoner review board, stated that Gibson, then 44, had served his time, and nothing could be done to prevent his release.

Gibson's sister, Pamela Will of Griggsville, Illinois, argued that the media had exploited her brother, and that the community needed to move on. In contrast, Lolela Freeman, Marcella's mother, believed that the people of Decatur, who had opposed Gibson's release for years, needed to be aware of his return to the community.

As the years passed, Michael attempted to rebuild his life. He found work at Claire's restaurant and even discovered a passion for fishing and playing the guitar. But despite his efforts to move on, the shadow of his past continued to haunt him. The community, too, struggled to come to terms with his presence. Many had opposed his release, and the knowledge that he was living among them again was a constant reminder of the horror he had inflicted.

And then, on Halloween day, 2021, Michael's life came to an abrupt end. At the age of 63, he passed away at St. Mary's Hospital in Decatur, leaving behind a legacy of pain and sorrow. The news of his death brought a mix of emotions to the Freeman family.

While some may have felt a sense of relief, others were left to grapple with the unanswered questions that had haunted them for so long.

Why had Michael committed such a heinous crime? What had driven him to

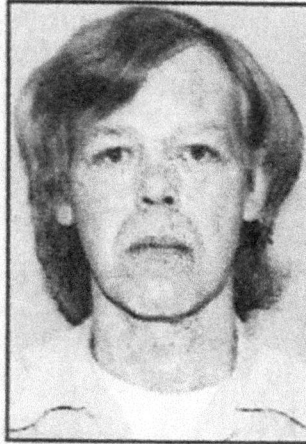 

Gibson, 2002   **Gibson, 1976**

take the lives of two innocent young girls? The lack of motive had always been a source of frustration and anguish for the family, and now, with Michael's passing, they would never have the answers they so desperately sought.

As the town of Decatur mourned the loss of a life, they were also reminded of the devastating impact that Michael's actions had on the Freeman family. The scars of that tragic event would never fully heal, and the memory of Marcella and June would forever be etched in the minds of those who knew them.

In the end, Michael's story served as a haunting reminder of the devastating consequences of violence and the importance of seeking justice for those who have been wronged. Though he may have served his time, the pain and suffering he inflicted would continue to reverberate through the lives of those affected, a somber reminder of the darkness that lurks within humanity.

HAUNTED SENTINEL
1.4.3. (I LOVE YOU!)

SUSAN A. JACOBUCCI

My hometown, Scituate, located some twenty-five miles southeast of Boston, Massachusetts made *Smithsonian Magazine's* 2024 annual list of America's Best Small Towns to Visit. And it is no wonder why this town, incorporated in 1636 with its rich maritime history, vibrant harbor, picturesque sandy and rocky beaches, and recently restored lighthouse earned this distinction. The Old Scituate Light, freshly painted white with a new shiny copper lantern room, is one of the town's brightest and busiest tourist attractions and is easily accessible along a paved coastline cottage-clad road with free parking. The twenty-five-foot tall, octagonal lighthouse with attached keepers' cottage features walkable jetties and paths, benches, and spectacular ocean views. The lighthouse is one of the country's oldest. It was built in 1811 to warn ships from running aground the rocky coastline; however, Old Scituate Light is not the only visible lighthouse in the town. There is a second, one with a tragic history and supernatural past.

In stark visual contrast to the Old Scituate Light, Minot's Ledge Light, constructed out of dull dovetailed grey granite blocks, is a one-hundred-and-fourteen-foot circular tower situated about one mile offshore in the chilly waters of the Atlantic. The structure emotes a feeling of isolation; the only way to get a close-up view is by boat. The solitary cylindrical lighthouse tapering from its base to its lantern stands like a shadowy sentry amongst the waves. Its

beacon protects mariners from grounding and destroying their ships against a jagged rocky ledge that runs along the shoreline between the towns of Scituate and neighboring Cohasset. This ledge formerly known as Conahasset, which translates to a "long rocky place" was named after the village and of the people who inhabited the area at the time of European settlement. Native people brought gift offerings to the ledge to placate a spirit they believed dwelled within it who was responsible for creating catastrophic storms that occasionally plagued the area. The ledge was renamed after George Minot, a wealthy Bostonian who lost one of his ships against it during a storm in the mid-1700s. There is a long history of storms that have impacted the area. Minot's Ledge claimed forty ships between 1832 and 1841 and took forty lives between 1817 and 1837, which was the impetus in 1847 for construction of a lighthouse in that location. Minot's Ledge Light is a rock lighthouse built upon the ledge.

The rock lighthouse that stands today is not the original. The initial was an iron skeletal lighthouse, a modern design drawn up by the architect Captain William H. Swift. The lantern room with oil lamps and reflectors and keeper's quarters were built seventy-five feet high above the ocean surface on top of nine iron piles that were sunk five feet into and cemented in the ledge. It took three years to complete construction. Workers could only build during calm weather and at

could hear the pilings moan from the stress of the incessant unforgiving waves. Dunham questioned the integrity of the structure and recounted his unnerving experiences during a fierce April storm as "an ugly sea which makes the lighthouse reel like a drunken man." He wrote to the Lighthouse Service and requested they strengthen the structure. The Lighthouse Service ignored Dunham's request. In a late summer storm, his spooked cherished cat dove over the side of the lighthouse and perished in the sea. Dunham resigned from his post after just nine months on the job. John Bennett a retired seasoned English sailor replaced him. Bennett had two assistants, John Wilson, a sailor, and Joseph Antoine, a Portuguese seaman. Shortly after Bennetts' tenure he questioned the lighthouse's structural integrity. He advised that the bent crosspieces between pilings should be repaired and raised issue for his safety and for his staff. The lighthouse architect Captain Swift reassured Bennet that the structure was sound and sent a repair crew out to straighten the bent cross braces.

Bennett and his assistants endured an intense stormy winter, but they could not anticipate or be prepared for what would occur in April of 1851. Having lived in Scituate and experienced multiday storms such as the "Blizzard of 78" and the "No

short durations since the ledge is only partially visible above the water line at low tide. The lighthouse lamps were lit on New Year's Day in 1850. Author Henry David Thoreau, described the finished product as "an eggshell painted red and placed high on iron pillars, like the ovum of a sea monster floating on the waves." The architect theorized that the innovative lighthouse design would allow ocean waves to pass harmlessly through the open structure; however, the lighthouse keepers described just the opposite.

Two or three male attendants staffed Isolated lighthouses and towers referred to as "stag lights." The first Minot's Ledge Light keeper, Isaac Dunham, whose prime duty was to keep the oil lamps lit, the wicks trimmed, and the reflectors clear, reported violent gale winds rocked the lighthouse from side to side and said he

Name *Storm of 1993*" later renamed "The Perfect Storm" I can attest to the ferociousness of the Atlantic Ocean. The storm that hit the area on April 16, 1851, showcased the ocean's fury. The storm was fierce and featured gale force winds, unusually high tides, and seas, struck with full rage during a full moon. The storm savaged the southern New Hampshire and eastern Massachusetts coastline.

Before the onslaught, Bennet had rowed ashore to retrieve supplies leaving Antoine and Wilson to tend to the lighthouse. Because of the intensifying swells at the time of Bennett's return trip, he remained onshore. From the beach he watched waves swell to catastrophic heights and saw the lighthouse sway back and forth in the wind during the night. He was proud of his assistants. Antoine and Wilson kept the lamp lit and rang the fog bell maniacally as the lighthouse pilings slumped. After midnight, shoreline dwellers could no longer see the lamp lit; the fog bell grew deafening silent.

Mangled iron pilings on Minot's Ledge were all that remained of the lighthouse at daybreak. Debris from the structure, equipment and furnishings, and the keeper's personal belongings littered the shoreline. Joseph Antoine's body washed ashore on Nantasket Beach in the neighboring Town of Hull, and John Wilson's body was on Gull Island off the coast of Cohasset. It was hypothesized that Wilson swam to the island from Minot's Ledge but fatefully died from exposure.

This tragedy did not dissuade the newly established Lighthouse Board from constructing a second light. Instead of replacing Minot's Ledge Light with a similarly constructed iron skeletal lighthouse, the design which also had catastrophic results at Bishop Rock in the Isles of Scilly off the coast of England, they implemented a more conventional design. The new Minot's Ledge Light, which is the cylindrical structure that stands today, is a solid construction from its foundation up to forty feet except for a small well for drinking water. Workers reported besides dealing with the wind and rough surf during the construction phase of the tower, a supernatural force made its presence known. "A spectral figure was seen clinging to the base of the ladder."

It took five years to complete the structure, and the lighthouse officially went into service in November of 1860. Even though the new light was equipped with innovative technology, a Fresnel Lens that produced a brighter beam of light, oil lamps used to fuel the light were used and human hands continually needed to fill and maintain them. The living conditions at the new lighthouse were not ideal. The storeroom, the assistant keeper's room, the keeper's room, the living area with kitchen, were usually dark and damp, one room to a floor stacked on top of one another with rare daylight trickling in through sporadically placed "heavy barred glass" windows. On top of these rooms lay the light, here a keeper was on duty throughout the night. Keepers were tethered to their lighthouse home and when they had the opportunity to stretch their legs outside of it, they could not go far on their constrained rock wasteland. Keepers felt isolated from mainstream society. They depended on each other and on the arrival of unreliable boat crews bringing supplies for companionship and longed for their sporadic trips to the mainland to connect with their family and community.

Keepers continuously endured the roar of the winds and waves that would "shiver and vibrate" their tower home. From 1860 to 1947, there were approximately fifty-seven individuals stationed at Minot's Ledge Light as keepers and assistants. Few keepers did not seem to mind the solitude, but it was difficult for most with one keeper lasting just five days on the job. Another keeper became deranged during his assignment at the light. Keepers and their assistants recounted mysterious experiences at the lighthouse. Perhaps the psychological warfare the elements played on their psyche had something to do with it. Keepers and their assistants reported hearing unexplained noises including groans, the fog bell ringing even though it was not activated, tapping against the granite lighthouse walls, pounding on its doors, disembodied voices, and the clanging on pipes which were reported to be the manner Antoine and Wilson used to communicate with one another when tending to the light. There were also spectral sightings, especially of two ghostly figures in the lantern room

which keepers believed were the spirits of Antoine and Wilson. There were also claims that maps were mysteriously filed and logs completed, and the Fresnel Lens and lantern windows were already polished before the keepers began their task!

In 1894, workers installed a rotating mechanism at Minot's Ledge Light to convert it to a flashing light. The light flashed a one, four, three pattern that has been ironically "interpreted by lovers alongshore as "I love you" because of the same number of letters in the words that correspond to the flashing sequence. In 1947 the tower was automated. Even though keepers were permanently relieved of their duties since that year passing fishermen and boaters claim to see a spirit many believe to be Joseph Antoine clinging to a ladder that is attached to the outer wall of the tower yelling warnings in Portuguese to stay away from Minot's Ledge. Some allege to see lanterns swaying inside the abandoned light. Others claim to hear cries for help coming from near the base of the tower and some report seeing and hearing "a very wet and anxious cat standing on the station's boat landing and squalling at the top of its lungs."

Minot's Ledge is a mysterious location where people have experienced supernatural occurrences long before the construction of a lighthouse. Perhaps since the ledge is a place where the balance between life and death is perilous at best and because of this realization the occupants of the area have always passionately revered and respected the location. The native inhabitants developed a relationship with the area due to their experiences. They offered gifts to the dweller of the ledge to safeguard their community from its wrath. And the lighthouse keepers also maintained a relationship with the ledge, one in which it was their solemn duty to alert others of the dangers of the ledge. Some keepers literally sacrificed their lives for the safety of their community; while others who survived their watch gave up their way of life while on duty. Otherworldly encounters continue to be ongoing at Minot's Ledge which include sightings of the phantom keepers and their lanterns.

In taking photographs of the lighthouse for this article, I had my own unique experience along the Cohasset shoreline adjacent to Government Island which features a replica lantern room constructed from some of the granite blocks workers removed from the Minot's Ledge Light during renovations in the 1980s. As I was getting ready to take photographs I heard a crow cawing. The cawing intensified; the calls grew closer. Still seated in my vehicle, I

glanced up and noticed a shiny black crow perched on a granite fencepost. I got out of my vehicle and managed not to spook the bird. The crow flew closer and perched on top of a parking sign directly in front of me. It kept up its banter with various call sounds as if giving a warning. The crow became silent and seemed to be curious about what I was up to then it flew off. Crows are known for their watchfulness and always have a sentinel posted, just like the light keepers. Perhaps this crow was continuing the light keepers watch.

DEAD WRINGER
THE MURDER OF VERA HENRY

JAKE BONNETT

AFTER READING THE MORNING PAPER ON MAY 25TH, 1919, THE COMMUNITY OF DECATUR, ILLINOIS, WAS LEFT WITH AN AWKWARD TENSION IN THE AIR AS THE NEWSPAPER PUBLISHED AN UNUSUAL NOTICE IN THE CLASSIFIEDS.

Harry Youtz boldly declared that he would no longer be responsible for any debts incurred by his wife, De Etta. The announcement sent ripples through town, igniting gossip and speculation about a troubled marriage. De Etta, known for her charm and resilience, found herself at the center of a scandal she never asked for.

As the months passed, the cracks in their relationship widened. On April 7th, 1920, De Etta filed for divorce on the grounds of desertion, putting Harry on trial stating that he had "joined up with a soul mate and went to Detroit," taking their four-year-old son with him. The town was divided; some sympathized with De Etta, a mother fighting for her children, while others whispered about her perceived failings as a wife. In the end, she was granted the divorce and custody of her two youngest children, but the scars of abandonment lingered, shaping her future relationships and fueling an inner turmoil that would later spiral out of control.

A decade later, in June of 1930, a woman named Vera Henry received accolades for her contributions to public service, bringing attention to the quiet yet resilient women of Decatur. Among them

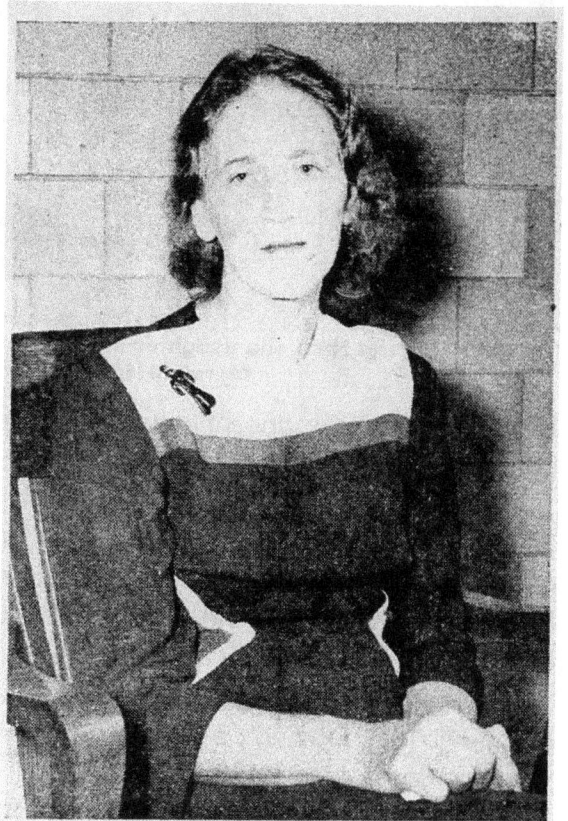

De Etta Ham, the publicly embarrassed wife of Harry Youtz, who worked hard to salvage her social status in Decatur in 1930.

was De Etta, who had reinvented herself as a devoted mother and aspiring socialite. Yet, shadows from her past remained, particularly as her daughter, Harriet Ham, a saleswoman at Neumode hosiery shop, began courting Marshall G.

(Left) Harriet Ham, the daughter of De Etta Ham and (Right) Marshall Henry

As the sun set on the quiet streets of Decatur on August 16, 1943, the lifeless body of Vera Henry, 46, was discovered in the basement of 1773 Clay Street, the home of De Etta and William Ham. Vera was found nude, badly beaten, with an oilcloth wrapped tightly around her battered head. A frantic call from her mother to the police at 1:00 AM set the wheels in motion, leading to the grisly discovery just hours later.

The scene was horrifying: signs of a violent struggle marred the living room, blood trailing from the scene of the crime to the basement where Vera's body lay slumped on the steps leading to an entrance. A bloody trail revealed an attempt to drag her lifeless form, while her blood-soaked clothes were found discarded in a pile behind the furnace, hidden away as if to erase the evidence of a heinous act.

When asked if Vera had been at her home that night, she denied it vehemently. But as the investigation unfolded, it became clear that the shadows of her past and a growing jealousy over her daughter's choices had consumed her. Neighbors reported hearing sounds of violence around 6:00 PM, just hours after De Etta had sent her son to invite Vera over at 3:00 PM. When pressed, De Etta first denied sending her son, only to later

Henry, a switchman at the Wabash Railroad.

The couple's engagement on April 28th, 1942, seemed to offer De Etta a glimmer of hope. Perhaps Harriet's happiness could mend the broken pieces of her own heart. But fate had other plans. Just a few months later, Marshall enlisted in the Marines, leaving De Etta to grapple with her unresolved emotions.

On November 11th, 1942, as Marshall trained in San Diego, he attended a Christmas party where he met the glamorous Lana Turner and fellow Marine, Bob Crane. The air of excitement and danger hung heavy over New Bern, North Carolina, where Marshall and Harriet would start their life together after their wedding on March 2nd, 1943.

admit it, though she maintained she never invited Vera to her home and had not seen her that day.

The evidence painted a damning picture. Bloodstains marred the wallpaper in the living and dining rooms, remnants of a desperate attempt to clean away the violence. Mr. Ham admitted to ongoing quarrels with De Etta, where her insecurities about his affections had flared into rage. It was a volatile mix of emotions that ultimately led to a fatal confrontation.

The next day, August 17th, a warrant was issued for De Etta's arrest. Friends and family recounted her disdain for Vera, and whispers of jealousy seeped through the community. It was revealed that De Etta's oldest daughter, Beth, had returned home that evening, intending to dress for a dance, but had overheard a troubling conversation that sent her away in fear. When she returned, the home was dark and locked, her mother's voice urging her to stay away until later that night.

With every detail that emerged, the horror of the crime deepened. Vera had been standing at the door of the dining room when the first blow struck. It appeared there had been a struggle on the second floor, but the nature of the conflict was murky. Though no definitive weapon had been identified, nearby small bats and golf clubs suggested a frantic, violent altercation. In contrast, Vera's larger stature could not have been an advantage against De Etta's fury.

Vera Henry

In a moment of raw confession, De Etta revealed the depths of her jealousy. Convinced that her husband had eyes for Vera, the confrontation escalated to violence. "I grabbed the wringer of the washing machine and hit her on the back of the head," she said, her voice trembling. But it was the steel pipe, a disconnected piece from their gas stove, that had turned the scuffle into a gruesome murder. The sharp points had left Vera's face mutilated, a haunting image that

Police officer examining Vera's body, which was found at the bottom of the stairs in De Etta's basement.

would be etched in the minds of all who heard the tale.

After Vera lay lifeless, De Etta attempted to dispose of the body, shoving it down the basement stairs in a desperate bid to hide her crime. The brutal reality of her actions weighed heavily upon her. She burned the rug that had covered the body and stripped Vera of her clothes, trying to erase any sign of what had transpired. But once the adrenaline faded, the reality of her actions sank in. De Etta cleaned the blood-stained walls, her thoughts consumed with concern for her children: "What would they think of me if I should have done such a thing?" she repeated, the weight of her crime pressing down like an anchor.

The community, once warm and welcoming, became a cauldron of fear and suspicion as the news spread. Neighbors watched as police descended upon the Ham household, their whispers echoing through the streets, a cacophony of hearsay. Beth, terrified by her mother's actions and the sight of police at their door, had sought refuge with a relative that night, her trust shattered.

As the days turned into weeks, the investigation uncovered the intricate web of jealousy and resentment that had led to the tragic murder of Vera Henry. De Etta's confession exposed the raw, unfiltered emotions that had driven a mother to commit an unthinkable act against a woman she believed was trying to take her family away.

What had once been a family home was now a site of tragedy, and the question loomed large: could the ties of jealousy and betrayal ever truly be severed? In the end, it became clear that in the battle for love and loyalty, some would pay the ultimate price. The community of Decatur would never forget the name De Etta Ham, nor the brutal night when jealousy unleashed a torrent of violence, forever altering the lives of those left behind.

On August 18, 1943, De Etta Ham sat in the cold, sterile room of the police station, her heart racing after 30 grueling hours of relentless questioning. The weight of her confession hung heavily in the air, a mixture of fear and guilt. With trembling hands, she signed a statement that would seal her fate and shatter her family's world. She had killed Vera Henry, driven to violence by an all-consuming jealousy that had taken root in her heart long before that horrific night.

De Etta's full confession revealed how paranoid she had become, ignited at Harriet and Marshall Henry's farewell party. Amid laughter and well-wishes, a member of the gathering had read fortunes, claiming that Mr. Ham would meet a woman with dark, partially grey hair. The description had haunted De Etta, leading her to believe it fit Vera perfectly. Fueled by suspicion, she became convinced that her husband and Vera had shared intimate moments within the walls of their home, despite Mr. Ham's insistence that he had only seen Vera once when she visited with the family.

Their seemingly mundane life was fraught with tension; Mr. Ham, partially deaf from his military service, often failed to hear De Etta's queries, leaving her feeling isolated and insecure. In her mind, every unreturned glance and unanswered question became evidence of betrayal.

On the day of the murder, the air had been thick with hostility. As De Etta and Vera exchanged heated words, accusations flew back and forth. In a moment of fury, De Etta slapped Vera, igniting a physical altercation that escalated quickly. The two women fought

A police detective investigates the murder weapon – a steel roller from the washing machine ringer.

from the front room into the hallway, where De Etta, in a fit of rage, grabbed a roller from the washing machine wringer and struck Vera multiple times.

After dropping the roller, the conflict spilled into the kitchen, where De Etta seized a piece of pipe and continued the assault. Vera, though still conscious, was left bloodied and battered, De Etta asked if she would leave her husband alone and stay away from her family. Vera replied vehemently "I will! You and your family will never see my face again!". But the plea only deepened De Etta's rage. Misinterpreting Vera's words as a challenge to her marriage, De Etta lost all semblance of control and began to strike

Vera again with the sharp-edged pipe, each blow a testament to her unraveling psyche.

In the aftermath of the brutal fight, De Etta stood over Vera's lifeless body, uncertain of when exactly her friend had died. The reality of what she had done hit her with crushing weight, and panic took over. She attempted to wash Vera's head in a basin to stem the bleeding but soon realized the futility of her efforts. In a desperate attempt to conceal her actions, she wrapped Vera's head in a gunny sack, then used the oilcloth to ensure the blood wouldn't seep through.

Vera's funeral service was held the next day, August 19th, at Brintlinger's Funeral Home. A somber gathering of friends, family, and members of the Marine Women's Organization paid their respects, an outpouring of grief for a life cut tragically short. As Vera was laid to rest in Fairlawn Cemetery, the reality of her absence settled heavily on the community, a stark reminder of the violence that had shattered the peace of Decatur.

Amid the chaos, De Etta's three young sons—Harold, 6, Lee Andrew, 7, and Billy Jr., 8—were placed in the Boys' Opportunity Home following their mother's arrest. The innocence of childhood was stripped away as they were thrust into a world of uncertainty, their futures clouded by their mother's horrific actions.

As De Etta sat in her cell, the echoes of her children's laughter haunting her thoughts, she grappled with the consequences of her choices. The once vibrant family home had turned into a house of horror, where love had devolved into jealousy and violence.

In the quiet moments of solitude, De Etta was consumed by regret. She had thought she was protecting her family, but in reality, she had torn it apart. The questions loomed large: Was there a way to mend the ties she had so violently severed? Would her children ever forgive her? As the days passed and the trial loomed on the horizon, the truth of what had transpired that day would be laid bare, revealing the deep scars of jealousy and betrayal that would haunt not only De Etta but the entire community of Decatur for years to come.

On August 21, 1943, the community of Decatur gathered to hear the damning verdict from the coroner's jury. In a swift conclusion, they declared Vera Henry's death a premeditated murder, recommending that De Etta Ham be held without bond until a grand jury could convene. The somber atmosphere only deepened when new details emerged, revealing a diamond ring Vera had worn was missing, adding another layer of intrigue to the case.

The ring, known to be so tight on Vera's finger that it couldn't be removed without cutting it, was a significant piece of evidence. Harold Brintlinger, the county coroner, reported that Vera's ring finger was badly cut, the ring hanging precariously from her hand, as if its removal had been a struggle unto itself.

This gruesome detail suggested that there may have been an attempt to disfigure or devalue Vera, amplifying the brutality of the crime.

The most damning testimony came from William Ham, De Etta's husband. He recounted hearing her say ominously, "She would disfigure that beautiful mug of hers someday," raising alarming questions about De Etta's mental state and intentions. William painted a picture of a woman plagued by jealousy, confessing that De Etta often threw Vera's name in his face, accusing him of infatuation. He described the tension between them that day, admitting they had exchanged harsh words at noon and that he returned home to find her sulking, further emphasizing the strained dynamics of their marriage.

A police officer, who had discovered Vera's body, added to the prosecution's case, testifying that the washing machine roller, a key weapon in the murder, had been deliberately brought to the first floor. This detail suggested forethought in the planning of the attack, which had occurred shortly after De Etta's son, Lee, had delivered an invitation to Vera. Lee had told Vera, "Mother wants you to come over right away," leading Vera to question why De Etta hadn't come to her instead.

The jury deliberated briefly before returning with their verdict, reinforcing the conclusion that De Etta's actions were premeditated and intentional.

By August 25, 1943, the grand jury was scheduled to convene on October 4th, with De Etta still languishing in county jail, awaiting formal arraignment under the murder charge. As days turned into weeks, her mental state began to unravel, and her reflections grew darker.

On September 4, while sitting alone in her cell, De Etta shifted her focus onto her husband, attributing her violent outburst to his treatment of her. "If only Bill would not have said various things he did to me and would not have aroused my jealousy," she lamented. "This thing would not have happened, and now I could be doing the things I like to do instead of waiting here in jail." Her words were tinged with regret and a longing for a life she felt had been stolen from her.

"I sometimes wish that they would send me to the electric chair and get the entire thing over with as quickly as possible," she confessed, the weight of her crime pressing down on her like an iron shroud. "I have done wrong, dreadfully wrong, and I know it. There is nothing that can be done about it."

De Etta maintained that the murder had not been premeditated, asserting, "I only called Mrs. Henry over to my house to tell her that I was jealous of her and wanted her to keep away from my family." She recounted the moment Vera knocked on the door, a moment that felt preordained in hindsight. "When her knock came at the door, something told me not to answer. I started to go upstairs, but the devil must have prompted me to, and I did."

Her reflections were laced with a sense of cosmic injustice. "If there is a

God, why did He allow a thing like this to happen?" she questioned, the depths of her despair resonating in her words.

As the date for the grand jury approached, whispers of the trial filled the small town of Decatur. Residents speculated on the motivations behind De Etta's actions, some viewing her as a tragic figure, while others painted her as a cold-blooded murderer. Each day brought fresh gossip and morbid curiosity, as the community grappled with the reality that someone they had known had committed such a heinous act.

With her family torn apart and her future uncertain, De Etta faced the stark truth that her actions had irrevocably changed the course of her life—and the lives of her children. The court case promised to expose the darkest corners of her mind and the turbulent emotions that had driven her to commit murder. As the grand jury prepared to convene, the entire town awaited the revelations that would emerge from the courtroom, holding its breath for justice to prevail in a case shrouded in envy, betrayal, and tragedy.

The days leading up to October 9, were fraught with tension as the residents of Decatur waited for the next chapter in the tragic saga of De Etta Ham. On October 8th, news broke that Harriet Henry, De Etta's daughter-in-law and the daughter of the murdered Vera Henry, was seeking legal counsel for the first time since the charges were brought against Mrs. Ham. Marshall Henry, Harriet's husband, had visited De Etta just two days prior, a sign of the complex web of relationships that intertwined their lives, now forever altered by violence and loss.

On the morning of October 9th, the courthouse was packed, with the vast majority of attendees being women, many drawn by a mix of curiosity and empathy. As De Etta stood before the judge, she felt the weight of their gazes upon her, a blend of judgment and sympathy. In a whisper that resonated through the tense silence, she admitted, "guilty."

The judge, his tone stern yet compassionate, informed her, "Do you realize that under a plea of guilty, you may be sentenced to the penitentiary for any period from 14 years to life, or may be sentenced to death?" Tears streamed down De Etta's cheeks as she replied, "There is nothing else for me to do." But when the judge learned she had not consulted with a lawyer, he refused to accept her plea. A lawyer was appointed to ensure she understood the gravity of her situation and her rights.

The courtroom buzzed with anticipation as news of her plea spread. On October 15th, Mrs. Ham officially pleaded guilty to murder on eight counts, the case's hearing set for the following week. Spectators once again filled the courtroom, many women eager to witness the proceedings and perhaps find answers to the unanswerable.

By October 19th, 1943, the judge delivered his sentence: 150 years in prison. The courtroom brimmed with women once more; out of 250 people, fewer than 20 were men. De Etta sat, stunned, as the weight of her punishment settled over her like a suffocating blanket. The judge dismissed any claims of her unhappy home life as justification for her actions, and the prosecution refrained from seeking the death penalty. "Let her spend the remainder of her life reflecting on her actions," they argued, "on every anniversary of August 15th. That is the punishment fitting for such a crime."

In the midst of the sentencing, De Etta reflected on the farewell dinner that had unwittingly set the stage for the tragedy. She recalled the fortune telling that had hinted at a "dark-haired woman" entering her husband's life. Initially, she dismissed it, but as the party progressed, she couldn't shake the unsettling feeling that the prediction referred to Vera. "She had pretty clothes on and was standing close to my husband," De Etta recalled, "and I started thinking."

The courtroom listened intently as she recounted the confrontation with Vera. "I told her that I was jealous and wanted her to stay away. She said she had no interest in my husband but thought he was a nice man." The tension in her voice rose as she continued, "When I asked if it would be different if the children and I were out of the way, she wouldn't answer. That's when I slapped her."

De Etta's confession spilled forth as she described the scuffle that led to Vera's death. "As we scuffled, I got the washing machine wringer and hit her. She tripped me, and I dropped the wringer. Then I saw the pipe from the gas stove and hit her with it." Her voice cracked as she recounted Vera's feeble attempts to escape. "She said she would go out of my life and never bother me again. That made me think I was right about my feelings, and I hit her again."

Tears fell freely as she recalled her frantic actions after the murder. "I took my clothes and shoes to the bathroom upstairs and hid them," she confessed, the reality of her choices washing over her.

In a stark contrast to De Etta's emotional turmoil, the coroner, Harold Britlinger, took the stand to provide a chilling account of the condition of Vera Henry's body. He detailed the brutality of the attack: "126 stitches were required to close abrasions on the forehead. The right jaw and both shoulders were fractured. The head and shoulders were covered with abrasions and bruises." His clinical observations served as a stark reminder of the violence that had transpired in the Ham home, where jealousy had culminated in a devastating act of rage.

As the courtroom digested the evidence, murmurs rippled through the crowd. Women shook their heads in disbelief, grappling with the horrifying reality that one of their own had committed such a heinous act. Some expressed sympathy for De Etta, while others condemned her for taking a life and shattering two families.

The trial became a spectacle, an event that captivated not only the residents of

Decatur but also drew attention from the wider public. De Etta, once a woman bound by the ties of family, now stood as a cautionary tale of jealousy and betrayal—a reminder of how fragile the line between love and hate could be.

As the gavel fell and the sentencing concluded, the lives of all involved were forever changed. The impression of that fateful August evening lingered in the minds of those who bore witness, a chilling reminder that sometimes, the most terrifying monsters are the ones we invite into our homes.

On October 20th, 1943, De Etta Ham was escorted by deputies to the State Reformatory for Women in Dwight, ready to begin her 150-year sentence. The weight of her past actions pressed heavily upon her, yet, in that moment, she felt a strange sense of relief. The looming threat of the death penalty had vanished, allowing her to eat her supper and sleep peacefully for the first time in months. As she lay in her cell that night, memories flooded back—the constant strain of her home life, the sobs she had stifled over the years. Her husband, Bill, would often dismiss her tears, telling her, "People who cried like that were losing their minds." Now, those judgments felt distant, the sharp edges of her life dulled by the confines of prison.

As weeks passed, isolation enveloped her. On January 12th, 1944, after hours of silence in her cell, De Etta finally called out to a passing lieutenant. "Can I ask for a favor? Can I see my youngest children?" she inquired, her voice cracking with longing. The lieutenant's response was firm: "We are not in the habit of extending favors to people who do not cooperate with us. When you are ready to tell the truth, you will be in a better position to ask favors." This rebuff stung, but it also ignited a spark within her. Within moments, she began to recount her story to the authorities, the floodgates of emotion and regret swinging wide open.

Back in Decatur, life continued to shift in the wake of Vera Henry's death. On September 2nd, 1945, Will J. Ham sold the home where the tragedy unfolded to H.W. Moss, severing one of the ties to the horrific past. Yet, the shadows of that night lingered, casting a pall over the Ham family.

De Etta's time in prison became a journey of introspection. On May 12th, 1950, she petitioned for commutation of her sentence, arguing that she was not a murderer; the act was a result of temporary insanity. "I was of extremely nervous nature," she explained, "and it was easy to become emotionally upset over incidents that now appear to have been minor, but at the time seemed of major importance." Despite her pleas, Governor Stevenson denied her request.

Undeterred, De Etta attempted again. On February 19th, 1952, she informed authorities of her intent to apply for commutation once more. Yet, the state's attorney opposition loomed like a dark cloud over her hopes. Again, on May 13th, 1952, her petition was denied.

Years passed, marked by similar cycles of hope and disappointment. On September 10th, 1954, she made another request for a sentence reduction. Finally, on June 22nd, 1957, after much deliberation, Governor Stratton approved her request, shortening her sentence from 150 years to 99. De Etta was now eligible for parole after serving 33 years, a glimmer of light illuminating the long, dark tunnel of her confinement.

Tragedy struck the family again on January 15th, 1958, when William J. Ham died in California. His passing, while marked by sorrow, also represented another severed bond with her past. De Etta's focus returned to her own freedom; on June 11th, 1958, she petitioned for yet another reduction in her sentence. Once again, the state's attorney opposed her request. But on September 11th, 1959, in a surprising turn of events, Governor Stratton granted her another reduction, this time lowering her sentence from 99 years to just 51 years, making her eligible for parole the following year.

After 17 years and 10 days behind bars, De Etta Ham was paroled on October 22nd, 1960. The world beyond the prison walls had changed, but she was

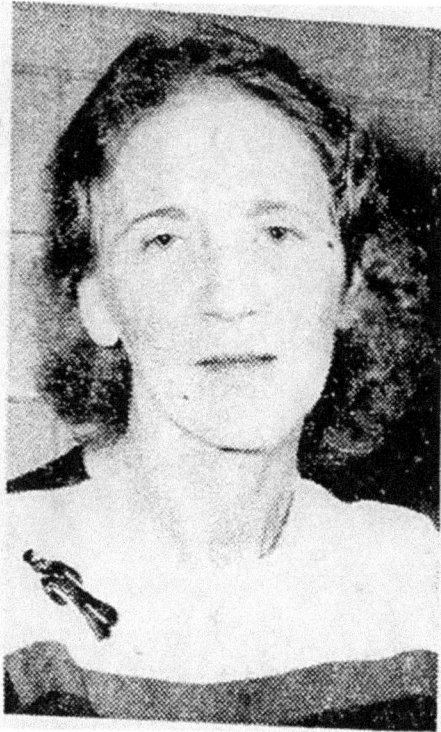

De Etta was released from prison in 1960 and lived for another 24 years before passing away in 1984.

determined to create a new life far from Decatur's prying eyes. She moved to Westminster, California, where her children awaited her. Here, she sought solace and anonymity, leaving behind the turbulent memories of her past.

In the years that followed, De Etta lived a quiet life, tucking her dark history away like a forgotten garment in the back of a closet. The harsh realities of her actions faded into the background, though the haunting memories occasionally flickered in her mind. Yet, she built a life for herself— a life defined not by her past but by the love of her children.

On June 9th, 1984, De Etta passed away at the age of 87. She was laid to rest in Westminster Memorial Park in Westminster, CA. A final chapter closed on a life marked by tragedy, jealousy, and violence. The whispers of her past lingered, weaving through the memories of those who knew her and those who were drawn to the story of a woman who had once let jealousy consume her. In the quiet of Westminster, the memories of that warm August day in Decatur remained, a poignant reminder of the ties that bind us, for better or for worse.

SHADOWS OF A TRAGEDY

THE HAUNTING LEGACY OF THE MAURY COUNTY JAIL FIRE

WENDY HAYWOOD ESKEW

MY HOMETOWN OF COLUMBIA, TENNESSEE IS STILL A SMALL TOWN, BUT FORTY-SEVEN YEARS AGO IT WAS EVEN SMALLER. EVERYONE KNEW MOST EVERYONE ELSE AND THE SAME FAMILIES HAD LIVED IN THE AREA FOR GENERATIONS. EVERYTHING SEEMED TO MOVE SLOWER THEN, ESPECIALLY ON SUNDAYS. THAT DAY WAS RESERVED FOR CHURCH AND FAMILY. COLUMBIA IS THE COUNTY SEAT OF MAURY COUNTY; THEREFORE, IT IS THE SITE OF THE MAURY COUNTY JAIL.
THIS IS WHERE OUR STORY BEGINS.

The jail was constructed in 1963 on the site of the former, outdated facility. It was constructed in the shape of a cross with four wings. The north wing was called "the workhouse" and had ten cells, five on either side, that housed four prisoners each. The west wing contained a storage area, the kitchen, laundry room, and two maximum security two person cells. The east wing contained two "drunk tanks" and a padded cell for disruptive prisoners. There were also two eight-person cells one of which housed any female prisoners. The south wing contained the sheriff's office and other administrative rooms. The center of the building was where the dispatch office was located. All of this amounted to 7200 square feet.

On June 26th, 1977, it was a hot Sunday. And Sunday was visitation day at the jail. It began at one o'clock sharp and lasted one hour. There were fifty-three inmates at the time. There were fifty males and three females. Thirty-nine people were visiting their loved ones. Two deputies were on duty along with an investigator, dispatcher and jailer. So, a total of ninety-seven people were in the building that day. The sheriff was out of town on police business. The only visitor locked in a cell was a gentleman visiting his son in one of the maximum-security cells. Sometimes inmates were allowed to visit outside and, in some cases, even go to church with their families, but there had been a jail break earlier in the week, so things were stricter on that day.

Everything was going per usual when at 1:55 pm, just five minutes before the visitors would be leaving, a fire was intentionally set in a padded cell. The cell was occupied by a sixteen-year-old runaway from Wisconsin.

He had been picked up hitchhiking a couple of days before. He has run away from a reform school where he had set fires previously. He was originally in one of the drunk tanks to keep him sequestered from the adults while he awaited extradition back home. He flooded the cell by stopping up the toilet, hence he was sent to the padded cell. It was there he bummed a cigarette and light from a visitor. He then set fire to the padding of the cell. The jail was constructed of fireproof material and the padding were supposed to be too. It was highly combustible and toxic. Only days before this the building was called "one of the better jails in the state" by the state inspection department. Despite this declaration, there were no sprinklers, fire extinguishers, and there had never been a fire drill conducted.

The teen began yelling for help, saying he was on fire, which caught the attention of a trustee. The trustee then seen smoke coming from under the door. He went for help immediately. The jailer on duty ran to open the heavy steel door. As soon as he swung it open a huge plume of fire, followed by thick black smoke exploded into the corridor. The smoke spread quickly and just as quickly; chaos ensued. The jailer was knocked to the ground and lost the only set of keys available. The other set was locked in the sheriff's office. The building was already dimly lit, so along with the dense black smoke, it became pitch black quickly. Officers yelled for everyone to get on the floor. A call went out over the scanner requesting all emergency personnel to report immediately to the jail. The fire stayed contained to the padded cell and was extinguished quickly bey the fire department. But the deadly noxious smoke persisted.

It took twelve minutes to find the keys, but the smoke was so thick they could not be matched to the locks. Every cell had its own key. The helpless inmates climbed the bars and begged for help while the visitors tried to find their way to the doors. Many were unable to locate the exits because of the thick smoke. So many people became dissimulated in the darkness. Two groups of visitors were close to an exit but ran the wrong way in the darkness and panic.

The inmates did whatever they could do to try to survive. They wet towels in the sinks and toilets to hold over their faces while they laid as flat as possible on the floor. One prisoner passed out wet towels to others, saving many lives while ultimately losing his own. The heat then busted the water pipes, ending even these measures. The heat outside was ninety degrees so surely it was even more unbearable inside. It did not take long for the cries for help to go eerily quiet.

Ambulances came from neighboring counties to help with the injured. Anyone who knew CPR came to assist. The funeral homes sent their hearses to transport people to the hospital. The hospital had just opened the new emergency room twenty days earlier and every employee

42 DIE IN JAIL FIRE

Smoke Sweeps Maury Facility

COLUMBIA, Tenn. — At least 41 persons were killed yesterday when a fire — believed deliberately set by a juvenile being held as a runaway — sent clouds of heavy black smoke pouring through the Maury County Jail.

About 40 other persons were [...]

The fire yesterday at Maury County Jail was covered by a team of reporters and photographers for the Tennessean. They included reporters Jerry Thompson, Connie Crowell, Kirk Loggins and Jim Sheppard and photographers Dale Ernsberger and David Fox.

Lockup System Possibly Hurt Rescue Effort

By KIRK HUNT

injured in the fire or in the massive efforts to combat it.

AT LEAST 34 of the dead were prisoners who were trapped in their cells as the smoke boiled through the one-story, concrete structure. Officials said eight other victims were visitors to the jail at the time of the 1:45 p.m. blaze. They said four members of one family were believed killed in the rush to escape the fire, and the dead included two women.

Fire officials attributed all the deaths to smoke inhalation.

Prisoners shook their bars in fear and desperation and shouted for guards to unlock their cells as the smoke filled the jail.

The guards reacted by frantically trying to release the inmates — but the rescue effort was hampered, fatally so, when some 15 visitors to the jail collided with a deputy in their rush to escape, causing [...]

was called in to help. Haywood's Wrecker and Gray's Wrecker came with sledgehammers to break windows and holes in the stone walls, hoping to let out the toxic smoke and let in fresh air. My uncle owned Haywood's Wrecker, and my father worked for him. My Dad threw a sledgehammer at the high windows in the back to break them. After this was accomplished, they hooked up the cables of the wreckers on the cell bars and pulled them out, making a way for rescue crews to get into the cells. My Dad said when he broke out the windows, the smoke that poured out was black with purple and green tendrils. They, along with others, went in hoping to find survivors, but unfortunately there were none at that point. They carried out dead bodies, many of whom they knew but could not recognize. The victims were covered in black, oily soot. Body bags covered the small front parking lot.

Seventy-five people were transported to the hospital. Only the teen who started the fire had burns. Five were treated and released, twelve were transferred to larger hospitals and sixteen were admitted. Many woke up in the hospital with no memory of how they got there. A temporary morgue was set up in the physical therapy room. The smell of smoke and death permeated everything. Forty-two people were lost. Only twenty of the fifty-three prisoners survived. All who perished died from carbon monoxide poisoning. One family lost five members of their family while another lost six. Medical personnel and funeral directors spoke of the awful site of forty-two bodies lined up in one room. Our little town became national news. Then governor Ray Blanton said it was "one of the greatest tragedies we've ever had in Tennessee".

In the following days, there were gaping holes, black soot, broken windows and debris on the sidewalk. Black, sooty fingerprints covered the outside walls. It is the second worst jail fire in America history. There was so much loss, heartbreak and disappointment. One young lady was only two days away from being released. Only two of the fifty-three prisoners were incarcerated for violent offences. Everyone else was in for public drunk, D.U.I, bad checks, simple possession, unpaid fines, etc. They all left behind family and friends who love and miss them. The survivors and emergency workers were left with trauma and horrible memories. My Dad said it was "the most horrible thing I have ever seen".

If any good came from this tragedy is that it did spark nationwide changes in the way jails are rated for safety. Fire alarms and drills are required now, and inspections are much more diligent. Because of all the mishaps there were lawsuits that dragged on for eight years.

The troubled young man who started the fire ended up spending eighteen months in prison after recovering from his injuries. He was then sent back to Wisconsin. He stated he never meant to hurt anyone, he just wanted out of the cell. The community just wanted him away from us. He still lives in Wisconsin and has never consented to any interviews.

The tragedy may not have ended that day. There have been several of the rescue workers who have passed from cancer in the years after the fire. There were so many noxious chemicals in that smoke. My uncle died of lung cancer ten years after the fire at the young age of forty-nine. He and others went into that smoky building and there were no protective masks to wear.

With so much fear and death in such a small space and in such a short amount of time it is no surprise that there have been reports of strange activity. The jail was renovated and reopened in the months afterward. It was not long after prisoners started reporting toilets flushing, and sinks turning on by themselves. Shadow people have been seen and random smells of smoke. One inmate thought he was dreaming when he seen a shadow figure crawling along the floor one night. That was until his bunkmate whispered "Randy, do you see that?". After that there was not much sleep to be had.

A bigger building was constructed in the late 1990s leaving the old building empty. It was quickly remodeled and turned into the Maury County Archives. The building looks nothing like a jail now. The renovations seemed to rile up anything still lingering there. People reported intense cold spots and feelings of being watched. People working outside the building have seen faces in windows that are too high for anyone to reach.

Once the county historian and his staff moved in, they started having experiences. They were even documented in an article in an October edition of the local newspaper. Most were just small things such as pens rolling off tables and misplaced things. One morning, the closed sign that featured a clock face that showed what time the building would reopen was found on the front counter with the time changed on it. A radio was kept in the breakroom, and it had a strange habit of changing stations and volume by itself. It became so unnerving, the staff decided to get rid of it. Another time, two of the employees were alone in the building when they heard a terrible crash that sounded like metal clanging. They investigated the part of the building where the sound came from and found nothing amiss. A former deputy later

came by and pointed out where things were located when it was the jail. The area the sound came from was formerly the kitchen and at least one person was found there. Eventually the incidents became few and far between. But the building just received another facelift in late 2024. It was also expanded and the section that was the jail is now used for storage. One cannot help but to wonder if any new strangeness has occurred.

The Maury County jail fire left its mark on the entire community. So many people were affected by that horrible day. Not a year goes by that the anniversary of the tragedy is not commemorated in the local papers. I want to believe that all those folks are resting peacefully and not sticking around the place that caused them so much pain and terror. There is a definite feeling of sadness that permeates the building. I do not think any amount of remodeling, or the passing of years will ever expel that.

LA PASCUALITA
THE REAL CORPSE BRIDE

BARRY COLEMAN

LET'S TAKE A TRIP "SOUTH OF THE BORDER, DOWN MEXICO WAY..." ALMOST MAKES YOU WANT TO BREAK INTO SONG, DOESN'T IT? BUT THIS IS A STORY THAT LIKELY ISN'T GOING TO MAKE YOU WANT TO SING.

If you cross over the border from El Paso, Texas, into Mexico, you will find yourself in the state of Chihuahua, the largest of the 31 states of Mexico.

Continuing on through the city of Juarez, and then further south, you will find yourself in the desert – eventually entering the desolate empty expanse known as the Zona De Silencia, or Zone of Silence. It's an area where few things function; no radios, cell phones, and you won't even hear the sounds of wildlife.

Journeying on will take you past a few isolated towns until arriving in the state capital, Chihuahua City. You're now about 245 miles south of the Texas border and a long way from home. It's a bustling city of about one million residents.

Oh, and by the way, if you wondered, the small dog known as the chihuahua is from this area. But if you use that name here, you will be corrected and informed the actual name of the dog is "Chihuaheno." A person from Chihuahua is called a "Chihuaenses." Of course, those from other cities like to jokingly refer to them by the same name as the little dog.

But back to our story...

If you continue through the outskirts of the city, you can look off to the east and see the huge Roman-style stone aqueducts that were built in the seventeenth century and are nearly three miles long.

When you reach downtown, you'll pass by the building that was once used by Pancho Villa as his headquarters. It's now a museum that contains the car, riddled with bullet holes, that he was riding in when assassinated.

Continuing into the business district, you come across Calle Guadalupe Victoria and you need to start looking for the somewhat nondescript shop at no. 803. It's called La Popular and it's a bridal gown store. Looking into the shop's display window, you can't miss the lovely, but controversial, mannequin that is dressed as a bride.

The mannequin is known as La Pascualita -- meaning "Little Pascuala" – although the original owner nicknamed her La Chonita, which referred to the Catholic Feast of the Incarnation, which is held on March 25, which was the same day that La Pascualita was placed in the window of the shop.

The shop was opened in 1930 by Pascuala Esparza de Perez, a woman who spent most of her time making her shop a success. The only thing she loved more than the store was her daughter so none of her friends or customers were surprised when Pascuala closed the shop and took the day off for her daughter Pascualita's wedding.

They were surprised, however, when the shop stayed closed for the next few days. Concerned about the friendly and inviting owner, that tried to find out what happened, only to have their worry turn to sorrow when they learned that her daughter, Pascualita, had died on her wedding day. Just before the nuptials were to take place, it was said she succumbed to the sting of a scorpion, or the bite of a Black Widow spider, depending on the source. Whatever it was, it was hiding inside her wedding dress.

The windows of the shop stayed dark for so long that people were surprised when the store reopened a few weeks later. They were even more surprised when they were met by Pascual, acting like her old self, but claiming that her daughter would always be by her side.

Meanwhile, people couldn't help but notice the new bridal mannequin in the shop window – and how familiar it looked. They soon realized that it looked just like Pascualita, the owner's deceased daughter. The mannequin was very lifelike and had small creases and wrinkles in her hands and very realistic skin, eyes, hair, and even veins in the legs.

As the news spread about the new, eerily lifelike mannequin, more and more curious onlookers came to see it for themselves. Many of them began to wonder if it was more than a mannequin – could it actually be the preserved body

(Left) The bridal mannequin that was placed in the shop window and (Right) Pascualita Esparza de Perez, daughter of the shop's owner?

of the deceased daughter? This rumor began to spread as more of those who came to see the mannequin started asking how an artificial figure could be so detailed. It seemed impossible that it could be a wax figure of some kind. They were convinced La Pascualita was a corpse.

After all, there have been many bodies around the world that have been publicly preserved or have never decomposed at all, including world leaders like Stalin, Lenin, Mao, and even Eva Peron of Argentina. Of course, their bodies were maintained to appear as if they hadn't decomposed. There are also those who have reportedly not decayed at all.

Many religious figures have been said to miraculously retain lifelike qualities.

A closeup of La Pascualita's hand, showing the fine lines ands creases that seemed too detailed to be artificially created by many of those who came to see her.

Known as "Incorruptibles," many have been beatified, a step before sainthood, by the Catholic Church. Usually on display in glass cases, there have been many eyewitness reports purporting strange phenomena. One of the most active has been St. Rita of Cascia (1381-1457). It is said she opened and closed her eyes for years. Her body was also said to have moved from one side of the case and then, a few years later, moved to the other. Documents of the witnesses to these events are kept by the Archdioceses of Spoleto.

There is also a blessed girl, Antonia Vici, who it was claimed raised her hand to bless a girl believed to be possessed by a devil when she was brought to her shrine.

There are also videos that exist online of a murdered Guadalajara girl – Santa Anasensia – who opened her eyes after being dead for 300 years.

But what about La Pascualita?

Believe it or not, strange events surround what may – or may not – be a bridal store mannequin.

One night, a taxi driver was taking a break and thought he saw a pretty woman in a bridal gown moving inside the moonlit window of La Popular. He was smitten and when he returned to the shop the next day, he was taken aback when he realized the lovely girl he'd seen walking past the glass was the mannequin in the show window.

Others claimed to see her move her fingers, her eyes, and some even claimed to see her smile. And why did her hands seem to show age, like a living person?

One story is told about a girl who was dying after being shot by her former suitor and when she looked in the shop window, La Pascualita saved her life by the miracle of her gaze. It seemed far-fetched, but her doctors said it was miraculous that she survived.

One of the more bizarre stories tells of a French visitor who, after seeing La Pascualita in the store window, fell in love with her, even after realizing that she was inanimate – or was she? The story goes on to claim that he was a magician and supposedly used a secret spell that brought the "corpse bride" to life. After that, stories spread around town that the couple was frequently seen around town, enjoying the moonlit nights, but returning the bride to her window before the sun came up.

Pascual Perez, the mother of the bride, passed away in 1967. Soon after her death, the stories of La Pascualita escalated, saying that she changed positions on her own, following customers in the shop with her eyes, and even leaving the shop to look for company on lonely nights.

The "Before and After" photos of La Pascualita after she was removed from the shop window during a restoration in 2017. Many who saw her after that claimed that she had been switched for a different figure while gone.

Of course, with stories like this, there are many inconsistencies. When researchers started to delve into the story, records showed that the shop's owner, Pascuala, had two sons – and no daughters.

Family members said that La Pascualita resembled the shop owner's sister, but city historian Dr. Acosta denied there is any truth to the story at all. He said the story is nothing more than a shrew marketing plot.

In 2017, La Pascualita was missing from the window for about nine months for an antique exhibit. When it was returned to the shop, many people immediately claimed that it was not the original mannequin.

Why would the owners have replaced it? Because it was claimed that while they were having the figure restored, it was found it was actually a preserved corpse after all, so it had to be replaced.

La Popular remains in business today and the current owner offers a pamphlet that recounts the entire story of the La Pascualita. Brides who are getting married can even stop by and have their nuptials blessed by the mysterious bride who also has her own Facebook and Instagram accounts.

Whatever her true origins, La Pascualita has become a local legend in her own right over the decades. It does seem unlikely that an embalmed corpse could remain intact in the Mexican heat for so many years, the current owner seems to know that she's at least good for business.

When asked for the truth about the famous mannequin in his storefront he simply winks and replies, "Is it true? I really couldn't say."

NO STONE UNTURNED

TERROR IN THE BRITISH COLUMBIA TRIANGLE

GINA ARMSTRONG
VICTORIA VANCEK

FEAR GRIPS YOUR ENTIRE BEING AND YOUR HEART RACES. THE ONCE SERENE SURROUNDINGS NOW FEEL MENACING AND UNFAMILIAR. YOUR MIND BECOMES FLOODED WITH A WHIRLWIND OF THOUGHTS—HOW WILL YOU FIND YOUR WAY BACK?

Every whisper and shadow heightens your anxiety, making you acutely aware of your vulnerability and isolation. The forest, which once seemed peaceful and inviting, now feels like a labyrinth of endless trees and undergrowth, and each path seems suddenly indistinguishable. The sounds of Nature, once calming and serene, increase your sense of seclusion making every snap of a twig or rustle feel like a potential threat. Reality presses down on you. Dread and terror set in as you face a nightmarish realization. You are lost.

Disappearing without a trace is a haunting thought that captivates the corners of our darkest imaginations. The shadowy phenomenon of mysterious disappearances has long piqued human curiosity. It is an unsettling reality that people can go missing anywhere. From the Australian outback to the bustling streets of New York, or a small quiet town in the prairies, countless individuals vanish each year around the globe. Their stories leave behind a chilling sense of the unknown.

During our research of strange creature sightings, local cryptids and UFOs in British Columbia, we started to come across disturbing stories of unexplained and unsolved disappearances. We were shocked to learn that according to recent statistics from the National Centre for Missing Persons and Unidentified Remains (Government of Canada), nearly 80,000 Canadians go missing annually, with British Columbia reporting the highest cases per capita. While many of these disappearances stem from abductions, wandering off, runaways, accidents and human trafficking, a significant number defy logical explanations.

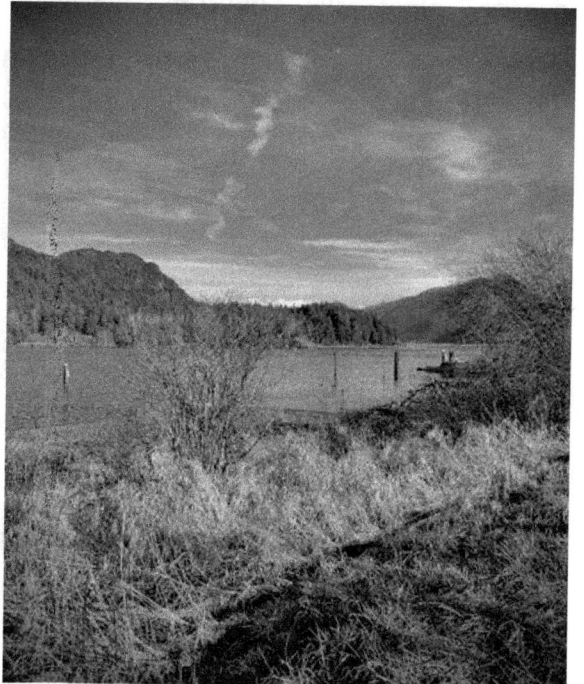

Delving into our research, we repeatedly came across an eerie phenomenon of people vanishing in BC's provincial parks. The conundrum of these disappearances is heightened by the sheer isolation of many of our national parks, leaving us questioning whether there might be something—or someone—lurking just beyond what we understand.

Many vast secluded areas of British Columbia have long been fertile ground for unsettling tales and local folklore—stories of supernatural occurrences, mythical creatures lurking in the shadows, or perhaps, even bizarre unexplained portals swallowing people whole. During our travels, people from local regions shared stories of strange evidence found in cases of missing individuals--cryptic footprints leading nowhere, strange lights in the night sky, unusual weather

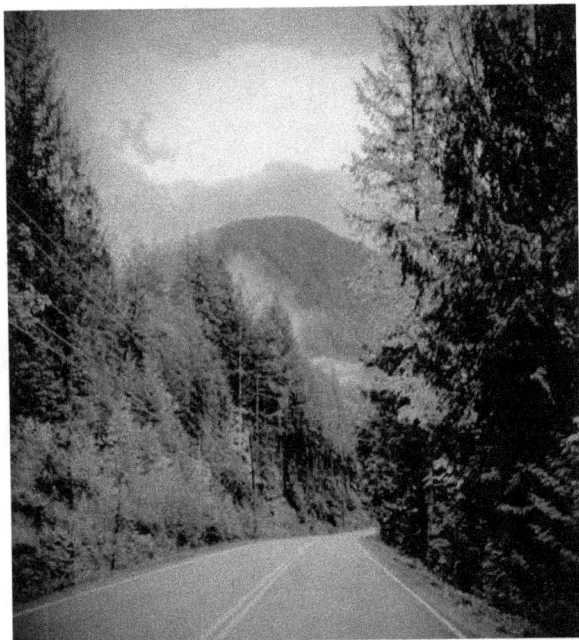

anomalies, and eerie sounds that echo through the forests signify a facet of these disappearances that can chill one to the bone. Even if you're skeptical about the supernatural, these stories might make you think twice before planning your next hiking or fishing trip to a popular forested spot. The unnerving prospect of otherworldly forces at work makes us ponder what truly goes on in these hauntingly remote expanses.

British Columbia's rugged terrain and dense forests have long been the backdrop for frightening tales and strange disappearances. One eerie instance dates back to the late 19th century when a logger named J.F. Gardner disappeared in the woods near Harrison Lake. Nestled in the shadowy valley of the Coast Mountains, Harrison Lake stretches almost forty miles long and over five miles wide, with its southern tip being about sixty miles east of Vancouver. The lake's eerie waters have historically been known to be the haunt of the elusive Sasquatch. During the gold rush, many a gold seeker met his demise by capsizing into its depths.

Gardner was known for his expert knowledge of the surrounding forest, but one fateful day he set off on a routine scouting trip and never returned. Despite extensive searches by fellow loggers and local authorities, Gardner vanished without a trace, leaving only whispered legends about what might have happened to him.

Another puzzling case from the 1800s involved the disappearance of prospector William Bryce. During the height of the Cariboo Gold Rush, Bryce ventured into the wilderness near Barkerville in BC's northern interior, hoping to strike it rich. Exploring the many labyrinthine trails, he was never seen again. Both men could have simply gotten lost, injured or succumbed to the elements. However, due to the lack of clues or clear explanations as to their whereabouts, their ghostly absences only added to the region's lore of haunted trails and supernatural forces lurking in the forests.

These disturbing stories reflect just a fraction of the enigmatic history surrounding British Columbia's vast wilderness. The eerie intrigue evoked by such stories continues to stir our imaginations, underscoring the haunting reality that some disappearances might never be explained.

For the past decade, one man has dedicated his life to delving into stories of the missing and has been chronicling mysterious vanishings throughout the United States and Canada. David Paulides, a retired San Jose police officer, has been investigating disappearances in remote areas which he attributes to unspecified unknown causes. In his ninth edition of Missing 411, in 2019

Paulides, now an author and researcher, explores the unusual disappearances specifically in BC's southern interior. One specific region has attracted public attention and stands out as particularly ominous as it holds the highest rate of missing persons. He dubbed the region "The BC Triangle" or "Canada's Bermuda Triangle."

The BC Triangle covers parts of well-known national parks such as Garibaldi, Pacific Rim, and the vast stretches of wilderness that remain largely untouched by modern civilization. Some notable areas and towns with this eerie zone include Whistler, Lillooet, Merritt, Kamloops, and Kelowna, all of which have been sites of unsolved vanishings and linked to several unsolved cases. Disappearances in this area frequently challenge local understanding, as people go missing under mysterious circumstances and are never located. Understanding the BC Triangle is crucial

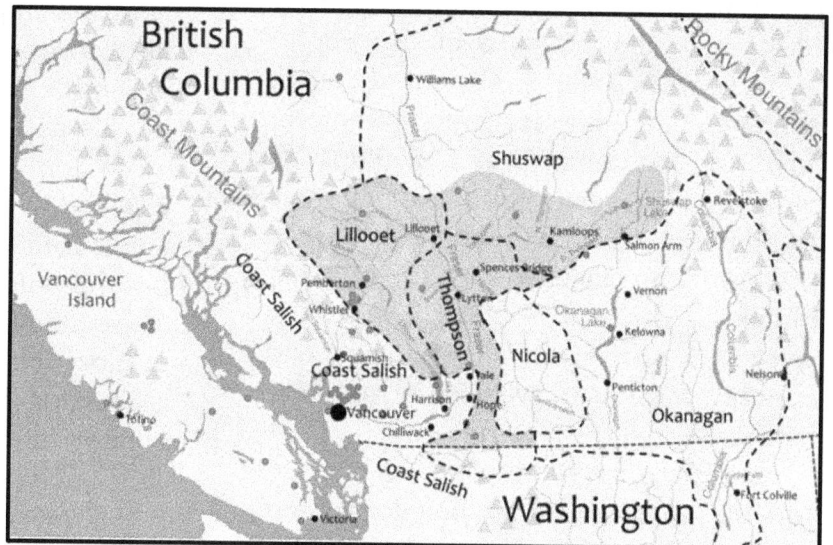

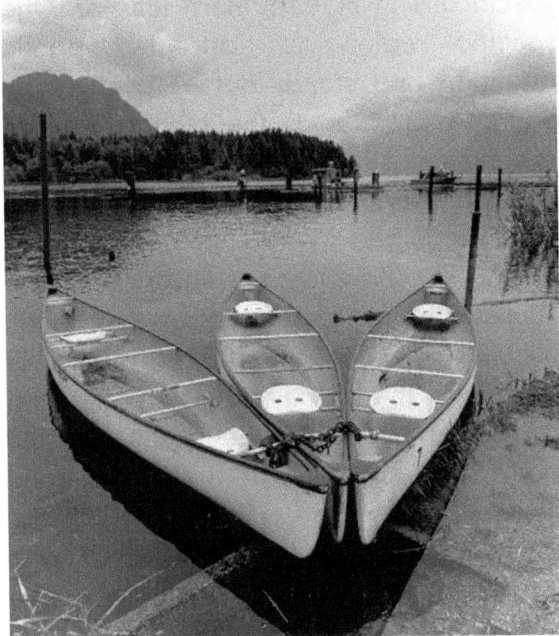

because it may hold keys to unraveling the mysterious disappearances within its expanse.

Several theories attempt to explain the eerie phenomenon within the BC triangle. Some suggest supernatural forces could be at play, the influence of geographic ley lines, while others speculate about the existence of undiscovered creatures lurking in the dense forests. Perhaps the most chilling are stories of people wandering through strange, unseen portals that transport them to other realms or dimensions. Such possibilities invoke a sense of foreboding and curiosity, leaving us with more questions than answers.

Grasping the intricacies of the BC Triangle is imperative not only for solving these baffling disappearances, but also for grasping the broader complex relationship between humanity and the untamed wilderness. The fear of the unknown haunts us but did it always? People once shared a profound bond with Nature and the woods, finding solace and wisdom in their surroundings. We once held a deep respect for our environment and lived in harmony with it. However, the advancements and technology of modern society have distanced us from the natural world, making us strangers to its mysteries. This unfamiliarity raises questions about what or who might be responsible for these disappearances within these secretive borders.

Through his investigative work, David Paulides has unearthed numerous eerie and perplexing cases that defy conventional explanations. When looking at BC Triangle cases he discovered that they had unsettling commonalities and strange occurrences that coincided with the vanishing events. He referred to these as profile points. One of the most chilling aspects is the frequent disappearance of people near bodies of water.

In July 1960, one such disappearance plagued the community of Red Lake near Kamloops. One evening, Maurice Masters and his wife went to town and left their 20-month-old daughter, Betty-Jean, outside the post office with two older playmates. They went inside for several minutes and when they came out Betty-Jean had vanished. The other kids couldn't recall any details of what happened and didn't give any clues as to how she disappeared. Extensive search efforts of the lake and nearby forested areas were exhausted, but the little girl was never found. Her disappearance sparked a vast array of theories from falling prey to a wild animal or that she simply wandered off. Many speculated more sinister possibilities such as foul play or supernatural forces.

Two and a half months after Betty-Jean's disappearance, another man went missing in the nearby area. Geza Peczeli, a 24-year-old Hungarian immigrant worked as a shepherd in Mount Baldy when he suddenly vanished. The RCMP said that it was almost impossible to conduct proper search and rescue efforts as the area was pummeled with an uncharacteristic snowstorm that made searching very difficult.

Paulides' second key observation in dealing with "triangle" region disappearances involves severe and sometimes anomalous weather conditions such as blizzards, fog, torrential rain, snow, hail, dust storms, and extreme temperatures. These adverse and atypical weather events often arise suddenly and unexpectedly after a victim vanishes, hindering initial search and rescue operations.

Clancy O'Brien's disappearance in 1966 remains one of the more mysterious cases in the BC Triangle. The nine-year-old boy and his family were visiting his grandfather's farm for a family wedding. At one point in the afternoon, while the adults attended the wedding, Clancy, his sisters and his teenage cousins went on an excursion up a nearby hill called Olson's Butte. At about 2:30 in the afternoon, Clancy left the group. Supposedly, he was headed back a short distance to his grandfather's house to get some wieners and bread so the kids could roast them by a fire. Clancy did not turn up at his grandfather's house and none of the adults saw him after he first set out with his cousins. Extensive searches ensued as word of Clancy's disappearance spread. The family, townspeople and local police armed with flashlights and dogs searched throughout the night. Efforts proved unsuccessful and there were no clues as to the boy's whereabouts. The lack of evidence and sudden nature of his disappearance sparked theories from accidental falls to more mysterious explanations. Having no definitive answers cast a sinister shadow on the haunting case. Several days after the incident, most of the family left to return home. Clancy's father stayed to search for his son for 23 days. The case is still considered open.

Over the years, locals in this area said they witnessed freak cyclonic winds create perfectly circular patterns in the marshy vegetation which grows in the shallowest parts of a nearby lake. And throughout the winter of 1974/75, a local man named Greg Irvine and his family were in the area near the Bonaparte River and came across huge footprints, found strange nests and hair samples, and heard nocturnal noises evocative of the legendary Sasquatch in the woods behind their cabin.

Another unsettling element is the suddenness of these disappearances, where people vanish seemingly in plain sight. Experienced hikers, young children, and seasoned outdoorsmen appear to be snatched away without a trace, leaving behind bewildering evidence like neatly folded clothes, or belongings set aside ceremoniously without a sign of struggle. In the Red Lake case, why didn't the kids playing with Betty-Jean mention an animal, a person or even her walking away? In all these cases, even sniffing dogs couldn't pick up the scent of those who vanished. These eerie situations beg

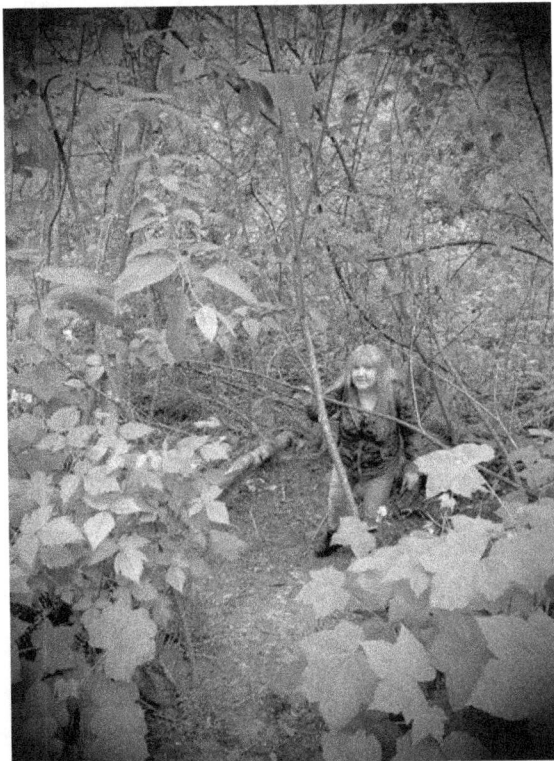

the question of how someone can go missing in mere seconds, not leaving even the slightest clue, often with others nearby who neither hear nor see anything out of the ordinary.

Paulides also notes numerous instances where recovered individuals, particularly children, are found in areas that are difficult or almost impossible to access. Individuals are found in mountain terrain that is high up or miles away from their last known location, often dazed and unable to recall what happened to them. One notable case involved a search and rescue operation that eventually found a missing person's body up high in a tree. The disturbing part is that the area had been thoroughly searched multiple times before the body was discovered. "Sometimes the location of the recovery has been searched dozens of times," Paulides wrote. "In one instance, the searchers had taken the same trail hundreds of times over the week hiking to where they believed the victim was located. On one day of the search, a tree had fallen across the path, and the young victim was later found lying on it. Nobody could explain the perplexing scenario."

In 2002, Brian Douglas Faughnan, an aerospace engineer, vanished near Whistler, BC while hiking Rainbow Mountain. He was found days later, miles from his last known location, with no memory of how he got there. Search and rescue teams were perplexed by his location because Brian would have had to traverse terrain that was nearly impossible to navigate within the time allotted, especially without gear and supplies. Surprisingly, he wasn't terribly disheveled or appeared like someone who had trekked tens of miles through dense, brush-choked trails. Did Brian encounter the mysteries of the BC Triangle?

Detailed documentation of such peculiar occurrences emphasizes the inexplicable and sometimes baffling nature of these disappearances, making us wonder about the true events that unfolded in those remote forests. These eerie profiles provoke many questions, feeding into speculative theories ranging from paranormal forces and cryptids to undiscovered phenomenon lurking within the wilderness.

As if the bizarre discoveries we encountered weren't enough, during our research we stumbled upon, yet another piece of chilling lore woven into the shadows of BC's unique geography. Hidden among the ancient trees within remote forests of the Triangle region, people have reported seeing strange staircases. At first this might not sound unusual. During our own trips into the local forests, we've seen remnants of old buildings or evidence of foundations left behind by early pioneering settlements. We've come across the weathered, crumbled structures or a few stone steps among overgrown paths where a homestead might have once stood. However, the stories of these mysterious staircases are quite different.

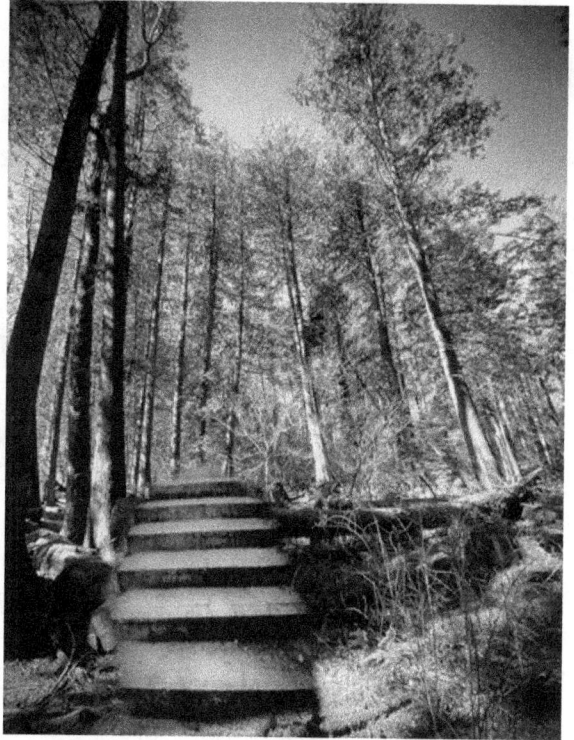

Bizarre phenomena of stairs or staircases found in the middle of forests have been shared in many online forums. The idea is both fascinating and spooky. The descriptions of what individuals come across are consistent. Imagine coming across a perfectly preserved staircase, often in pristine condition, leading to nowhere, deep in the woods. These staircases, seemingly out of place in nature, evoke a sense of dread and curiosity among those who encounter them. There are descriptions of all kinds of strange structures ranging from spiral, wrought iron staircases, sometimes concrete or wooden. One thing they all have in common is they look completely out of place and there is no evidence that they were once part of a nearby structure.

They stand alone like sentinels without an explanation of how or why they are there.

In a strange supernatural twist, these odd staircases have been tied to mysterious disappearances. Some legends suggest that these staircases serve as portals or gateways to other dimensions. It's said that stepping on or climbing them can cause a person to vanish into another realm, never to be seen again. Others claim the stairs are remnants of forgotten, otherworldly civilizations. Individuals who have witnessed these odd staircases claim that they emit a strange energy or frequency that compels creatures and people to want to climb them and once they do, they inexplicably disappear. The idea that these stairs might be linked to missing person cases add a supernatural layer to the enigma, making these accounts even more puzzling and frightening.

After finding out that Canada's very own Bermuda Triangle was in our own back yard, we set out to visit some of the towns in the mysterious region to see what we could learn.

There are logical explanations that can easily account for odd structures in the middle of the woods. We discovered a very unusual building on one of our own excursions while researching BC Triangle stories. About eight hours from where we live, our adventure took us to the small mining town of Likely, BC. With a population of about 350 people, the town is from a bygone era, and we had the thrill of staying at the very charming, historic, and haunted Likely Lodge.

The Likely Lodge is more than just a hotel– it continues to serve its original purpose as a haven for miners. Many who come to work in the local mines find temporary refuge here. And some, it seems, never truly leave. The lodge is home to a handful of lingering spirits, with the most notable being a mischievous, card-playing ghostly miner who haunts the pub and frequently triggers security cameras. During our stay, we encountered a myriad of unusual experiences–tales for another time, perhaps, but ones we won't soon forget.

The hospitable owners of the lodge, Christina and Kevin, told us about a mysterious and remote pioneer cemetery not far from where we were. We set out, rambling down an old, unmarked logging road. We navigated the rugged route with its choppy terrain and massive drop-offs, the car jolting and bouncing. Each jarring movement sent a shudder through the vehicle, and it made for a wild, and nerve-wracking ride. Eventually, we arrived at Keithley Creek Cemetery.

Despite its secluded location, the burial site dotted with humble wooden crosses and worn headstones, was clearly well maintained. As we wandered through this remote area, a small log shed caught our attention a short distance from the cemetery. Initially we assumed it housed gardening tools for the town's maintenance department. However, upon closer inspection, we noticed a sign on the front. To our astonishment, when we opened the door, we discovered a tiny library! Inside, it was clean and bright with shelves lining every wall, filled floor to ceiling with books.

We stepped inside to browse the overflowing collection and signed the guest book that lay open on a small student desk. What a magical find! There was something incredibly comforting about having a sign of civilization when you're conspicuously far off the beaten path.

Our peculiar discovery highlighted the possibility that remote areas might harbor items built or brought there by local residents or left behind by visitors. However, in the cases of the mysterious stairs, some witnesses claim that these anomalies vanish. Individuals who revisit the locations where they saw the staircases or pass the same trail again report that the stairs they once saw were no longer there.

Just like a puzzle with missing pieces, these disappearances captivate us because they challenge our minds and defy easy answers. In essence, the mystery of a disappearance fuels our curiosity and sense of wonder. It's an endlessly intriguing topic that resonates with some of our deepest fears and questions. Mysterious disappearances tap into our innate fear

Triangle encompasses parts of well-known national parks and vast stretches of wilderness that remain popular despite the region's reputation for various supernatural phenomena. While we are aware of dangers that can quickly arise in remote forests, the stunning scenery and marvelous backdrops of the wilderness act like a portal, drawing us irresistibly into its magical midst.

The BC Triangle's reputation as a hotspot for unexplained occurrences, mysterious orbs of lights, ghostly apparitions, Bigfoot sightings, and otherworldly beings will continue to call to our curious nature. Even if you're not a paranormal enthusiast, curiosity will lead you to peer into unknow realms—digging up the dirt, uncovering the layers, and testing the murky waters for answers. Sometimes when faced with the unknown, we must accept the unsettling truth that some mysteries are destined to remain unsolved. In the shadows of the BC Triangle, we find a haunting beauty in the unanswered questions and stories that linger.

of the unknown. When someone or something vanishes without a trace, it leaves a void filled with endless possibilities. Additionally, such stories play on our primal instincts and human tendency to seek patterns and explanations. We crave closure and understanding, but these cases deny us that, keeping us on edge and our imaginations running wild.

No doubt visitors will continue to hike scenic trails, kayak on tranquil lakes, or camp under the stars. However, as we have learned, these idyllic landscapes can hold a darker side. The very wilderness that guests come to explore can also become a vast, ominous maze where people vanish without a trace, encounter unknown creatures or confront mysteries beyond their comprehension. These elements add a chilling layer to the allure of these natural sanctuaries. The BC

And just a friendly word of caution—if ever you find yourself enjoying a peaceful hike in one of British Columbia's picturesque forests and you happen to stumble upon a mysterious staircase, we urge you to stay on the trail and just keep walking.

I HAD TO END THIS ISSUE ON "HAUNTED HOMETOWNS" WITH ANOTHER STORY FROM DECATUR, ILLINOIS — BUT THIS ONE IS PERSONAL TO ME. IT'S DEDICATED TO MY FRIEND, SKIP HUSTON, WHO PASSED AWAY IN EARLY 2025. EXCEPT FOR A SINGLE YEAR WHEN I OWNED IT, SKIP HAD OWNED AND OPERATED THE AVON THEATER SINCE 1999. SADLY, WITH HIS DEATH, THE AVON HAS CLOSED, BUT THE HISTORY, OF COURSE, LIVES ON.

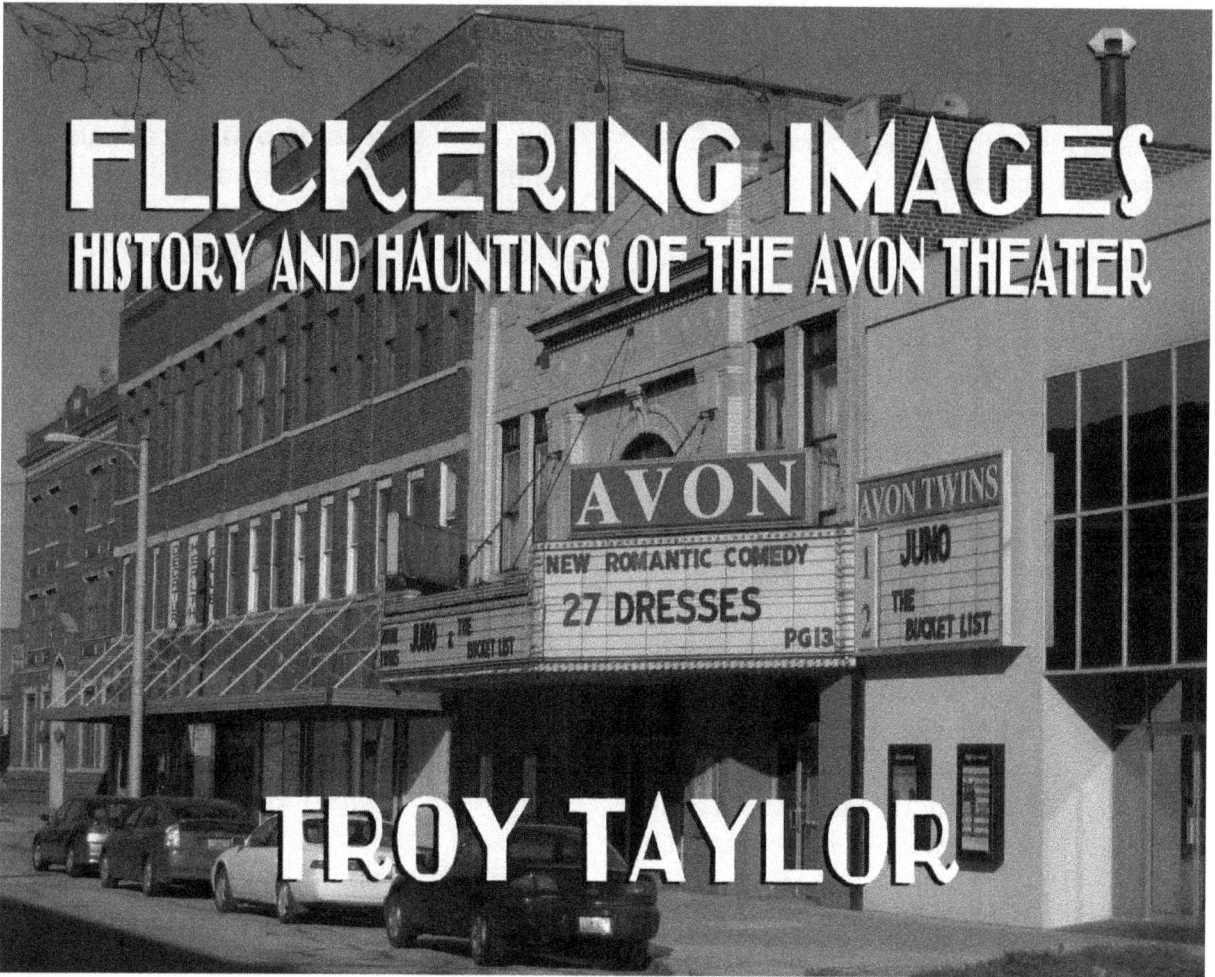

FLICKERING IMAGES
HISTORY AND HAUNTINGS OF THE AVON THEATER

TROY TAYLOR

The Avon Theater in the early days of moving pictures

Decatur's Avon Theater officially opened in November 1916. The Avon was a unique place in that it was a large, grand theater, on the scale of the scale of a vaudeville house, yet it had been constructed for showing moving pictures only. There would be some live entertainment and music later, with hosts appearing for the parade of films to follow, but this theater seemed like a folly to many. They thought it could never succeed, believing that moving pictures were a passing fad that would never last. But over the years, the American film industry has defied the odds and endured. Fortunately, even after several near disasters, the same can be said for the Avon.

Some of those connected to the theater believe that it's more than just luck that keeps the Avon Theater in business. They believe that it has something to do with the resident ghost, as well. This enduring spirit was around during the days of the theater's greatest successes and those who have encountered him can assure anyone that he still hasn't left.

In the spring of 1916, entrepreneur Joseph Allman announced plans for a brand-new theater in Decatur. It would be unlike any other in that it would be the city's first "movie palace," dedicated only to showing films. There were already several moving picture houses in the city, but most were cramped storefronts that operated on a shoestring. The Avon Theater -- as it was dubbed after a city-wide contest was held to chooses its name -- would have main floor and balcony seating for over 1,000 people, private boxes on either side of the screen, original artwork, and a grand design only found in the big cities of the era. Allman even convinced a friend, a student of Lorado Taft, to furnish statuary to be installed in niches in the theater. They would be joined by illuminated lion's heads, which would be mounted to the ends of each row of seats. Their glowing eyes would guide patrons in the darkness. Outside of the theater, Allman installed twin, seven-foot-tall statues to posts at the north and south ends of the building. A third statue, a woman reclining in the nude and holding a wreath, was placed above the whitewashed back wall of the theater, which served as the screen. Parallel with this figure, circling the auditorium, were bas-reliefs of women's heads.

The artwork and the decor were not the only things that make this theater special. The new film projectors were the best models available and an orchestra was scheduled to appear on a regular basis to provide musical accompaniment for the films. In addition, the theater was also equipped with a giant pipe organ that was electrically controlled. It was located in three different parts of the building so that it would be acoustically correct for the entire audience.

The theater opened on November 28, 1916. The first film was *Fall of a Nation*, based on a book by Thomas W. Dixon and it was shown to a standing-room only audience, packed into every available seat. In the months that followed, the Avon hosted dozens of well-received films, musical performances, and even fashion shows, presented by local dry goods stores. Occasionally, the theater would also host the stars of some of the films that were shown, especially those from the Essanay Studios in Chicago.

By early 1917, Allman had hired a manager for the theater, J.A. Carrier, and had stepped away from most of the daily

Opening night at the Avon Theater in November 1916

responsibilities of the business. To the public, things were going quite well with the Avon, but behind the scenes, the theater was a financial disaster. The cost of construction had nearly bankrupted Allman and he was soon forced to seek opportunities in addition to his beloved movie house. Even the best films, the music shows, and the personal appearances couldn't save the Avon and in August 1917, it was closed.

Later that same month, it was announced that an "outside firm" had leased the Avon from Allman. The former owner would still retain control over the building, but the business would be leased and operated by someone else. The new company announced that the Avon would remain dark until a "general overhauling" could be given to the place.

During this brief period, there was a lot taking place out of the public eye. The "outside firm" that was taking over the

Avon was Carrier Amusement Co., which was owned by C.E. Carrier, brother of the Avon's manager. What actual business arrangements were involved remains mysterious to this day, and it has been suggested that some underhanded dealings may have taken place in regard to Allman. All that is known about the building's owner is that after Carrier Amusement Co. took over the theater, Allman retired quietly to his farm in Monticello. He was never involved with Decatur entertainment again. The official word was that the Carrier Amusement Co. made it a practice to take over theaters that were in financial trouble and then to make those theaters attractive to investors again.

Carrier's company, which was based in Chicago and also operated five other theaters in Illinois, wasted no time in moving into the Avon. They announced a number of plans for the near future, including some additional remodeling. The interior was redecorated, and the paintings were removed. They also installed the first real lobby in the theater and lined a portion of the walls with marble and painted the rest in old rose with cream trimming. They also removed the center doors and replaced them with a box office that would allow tickets to be purchased from the street or from two side windows in the lobby. This box office would remain in place until 1972.

The Carrier brothers also announced that they would be making some changes to the theater's programming as well. Like most of the other venues in Decatur at that time, they would begin offering vaudeville shows in addition to films. The new policy would present two "quality" acts of vaudeville in addition to the films. The performances would be changed two times each week, on Sundays and Thursdays, and the films would be changed four times.

In March 1918, the Carrier brothers erected a new stage for the Avon and added small dressing rooms on either side. They hoped to lure larger vaudeville acts to the theater by removing the old stage --which was only 10 feet deep-- and putting in a much larger one. It was constructed from brick, concrete and steel and cost around $1,600.

But the Carriers would not remain in charge of the theater for long. Although they would continue their lease, the management of the Avon was taken over by R.J. La Voise, who had previously been the Carriers' house manager. His immediate boss, J.A. Carrier, had gone into the Army and was preparing to leave for Europe. In April 1918, he officially took over the theater's reins. He remained in that position through the war and in the troubling period that followed: the time of the Spanish Influenza epidemic. The epidemic led to the closure of the theater for a time -- along with all other public places in the city -- and saw many deaths in the city.

In March 1919, J.A. Carrier returned from Europe and announced that he would be selling the lease to the Avon

AVON THEATRE

Opens Under New
Management
Tomorrow
NEW PRICES

Week Day Matinee:
Adults 15c
Night, Sunday & Holiday
Matinee:
Lower Floor 25c
Balcony 15c
Children anytime 10c

WE STARTED IT

Biggest Quality Show in Central Illinois. | In Reach of Everybody

3 Acts of QUALITY **Vaudeville** and 7 Reels of PHOTO-PLAYS

Admission Always Main Floor **10**c | Balcony Any Seat Always **5**c

PERRY and DAVIS
The Palm Beach Rules

GEORGE and GOTT
A Blackland Farce

A BIG SURPRISE ACT

BESSIE LOVE IN **THE SAWDUST RING**
A Five-Reel Masterpiece

The Latest Two-Reel Keystone Comedy
We absolutely guarantee this to be one of the biggest treats ever offered to the Theater going public of Decatur, for the price.

AVON

A Leader By
Right--a Guide
to Others

The House of
Quality

Theater to a theatrical company that consisted of theater manager R.J. La Voise and several others. The lease, the equipment, and the goodwill of the theater were transferred to the new corporation and while the names of the new owners were not being released, the newspaper assured its readers that the company would "mean much to the city theatrically as it is prominent in the motion picture theater business." A month or so later, Carrier announced that he was leaving Decatur and was taking over the management of the Pershing Theater, located on the west side of St. Louis. The company that took over the Avon was the Mid-West Theater Corporation and for the next several years, it operated the Avon without incident, continuing with the business plan first instituted by the Carrier brothers. Programs at the Avon continued to be divided between films and vaudeville entertainment.

In April 1924, Mid-West merged with Balaban & Katz, which already owned five of Chicago's largest theaters --the Chicago, the Tivoli, the Riviera, the Roosevelt and the Central Park-- and this gave the company controlling interest in 50 theaters in the Midwest, including the Avon. They planned many changes for the theater and closed the Avon for more than two months for "elaborate improvements."

When it re-opened, everything with the theater had changed.

Despite the extensive plans made by Balaban & Katz, a small item appeared in the Decatur Herald newspaper on July 22, 1924. Apparently, Balaban & Katz had begun to have second thoughts about the viability of the Avon. Rumors were flying that W.N. VanBatre, the owner of the company, had traveled to Decatur to meet in secret with the managers of the Empress Theater, Gust and Christian Constan. It was said that the brothers were possibly interested in the theater and that negotiations were pending. On July 21, Gust Constan left for Chicago and it was reported that the deal had been finalized. When asked by the newspaper, however, Christian would not verify this. He only stated that he himself had not signed the necessary papers.

The following day, the rumors turned into fact. Balaban & Katz had abandoned their plans for the Avon Theater and had turned over the operation to the Constan brothers and their cousin, George Stevens of Chicago. The brothers had previously operated the Butterfly Confectionary, at 211 North Water Street, and had been part owners of the Empress Confectionary, across the street from the Avon Theater. They announced that the theater would be opened again in mid-August and from that point on there would be no more vaudeville performances. The Avon was strictly a movie house again.

The Constanopoulos brothers were Greek immigrants who became familiar fixtures in the Decatur entertainment business. During a more than 40-year span, they would manage and operate the Avon Theater, Rogers, Varsity, Castle Theater in Bloomington, and Times Theater in Danville. The four brothers, who shortened their surname to Constan, were Angelo, Gust, Christian and Theodore. They became very involved with the Avon -- especially Gust-- and truly moved the theater forward into the modern era. Their tenancy in the theater lasted the longest and had the greatest effect on what the theater has become today.

Angelo Constan was born in 1895 in Tripolis, Greece, and came to the America in 1922, joining two of his other brothers in Decatur. At that time, Gust and Christ were already operating their soda and candy shops and he went to work in the family business. Sadly, Angelo died at the age of only forty-seven in 1942.

Theodore Constan was born in Tripolis in 1900 and was the youngest of the seven children of George and Anastasia Constanopoulos. He came to America in July 1925 and joined his brothers in the theater business. As with all of the brothers, he became active with the local Greek Orthodox Church and was also involved with the American Hellenic Educational Progressive Association and served as a delegate to its national conventions. In 1945, he married Argero Tsevelekos and together they had five children. After he retired from business, Theodore moved to Denver, Colorado, and in 1992, he passed away at the age of 91.

Christian George Constan was also born in Tripolis and he came to Decatur in 1915. He was the first to join his brother Gust in business, and together they operated soda shops before getting involved with the Empress, the Avon, and the other theaters. Christ and Theodore were the last two Constan brothers in the entertainment business when they both retired in 1966. Christ remained in Decatur until his death at the age of 87 in 1978.

Of all the brothers, the most actively involved in Decatur theater --especially with the Avon-- was Gust. Born in January 1891 in Tripolis, he was the oldest of the brothers and he came to American in 1912. In 1913, he moved to Decatur and opened the Butterfly and the Chocolate Shop confectionaries. In 1924, he was instrumental in getting the family involved in the lease, and later the purchase, of the Avon Theater. He would remain active at the Avon --and with the Rogers and Varsity theaters-- until his death in 1965.

The Avon opened again on Saturday, August 16, 1924. For the next nine years, the theater prospered into the "talking films" era and the Constan brothers enjoyed much success in the city. In 1935, the theater closed again, but only for renovations as the financial troubles of the past seemed to be over. This period of remodeling marked the first major changes that had been done to the building since the Carrier brothers had taken over years before.

During the renovations, the balcony of the theater was completely rebuilt for the

FIRST RUN PICTURES POPULAR PRICES

AVON

HAROLD HUNTSMAN ORGANIST EARL VOYLES PIANIST Playing Special Illustrated Popular Songs

Continuous Today 1 to 11

Johnny Hines IN "The SPEED SPOOK"

With Faire Binney, Frank Losee, Edmond Breese and All Star Cast

SIXTY MILES OF THRILLS TO THE MINUTE!

SPEED — LAUGHS — ACTION — PEP

OH, BOY! WAIT TIL YOU'VE SEEN IT—

NO ADVANCE IN PRICES

ALSO

COMEDY — SPORTLIGHT — NEWS

price of $2,500. In addition, offices were added on the second floor, directly above the lobby. Across the hall from the new offices, and behind the new balcony, was the location of the men's restroom. It had always been a small, cramped space but was slightly enlarged and remodeled during this period. Later, a men's room would be added downstairs.

Another major change was also made to the projectionist's booth in 1935 with a door finally being added. Before this, the projectionist had to go up onto the roof of the theater, open a trap door, and then climb down a ladder into the booth. This

Gus Constanapolous

was done to keep the patrons of the theater safe in the event of a fire. During the silent era, movies were made using volatile nitrate film and under certain conditions, it could combust into flames. By not having a door on the projectionist's booth, the theater hoped to protect the audience should such a fire break out. The projectionist, I suppose, was considered expendable.

That same year, Gust Constan returned to Greece and while he was there, he married Vicky Platopoulou. She returned with him to Decatur. The Constan brothers still had two sisters and a brother in Athens.

The next several years in Avon history were largely uneventful, save for the outbreak of World War II and the death of Angelo Constan in 1942. The next set of changes for the theater came about in 1953, when the Avon was again renovated to keep up with the changing times. In addition to an expansion of the concession stand, a new screen was installed for showing wide-screen and 3-D films. And while 3-D movies, turned out to be a short-lived fad, the wider screen was an innovation that put the Avon ahead of other theaters in the city. The new screen was 12-feet high and 24-four-feet wide, which was eight feet wider than the previous screen. In order to install it, the old private seating boxes that were located in the front of the theater finally had to be removed. The new screen weighed over 300 pounds and was coated with a silver-tone finish that would not absorb the light. The screen was also perforated so that sound from the system behind it could reach the audience. The owners stated that the new wide screen "gives some illusion of depth and a great feeling of audience participation."

In 1965, after a three-month illness, Gust Constan passed away. Funeral services were held next door to the theater at the Moran Funeral Home and Gust was laid to rest in Fairlawn Cemetery. The Avon, Rogers, and the family's theaters in Bloomington and Danville were closed on the day of the funeral. It was truly an end of an era for the Avon Theater.

A few months later, on April 15, 1966, a 42-year period in Decatur entertainment came to an end with the announcement that Christ, Theodore, and Gust's widow, Vicky, were leasing out the Avon and their other theaters to the Kerasotes theater chain, based in Springfield, Illinois. With this acquisition, the chain boasted 53 theaters in Illinois. The small, family-operated business had come to an end and the Avon had been absorbed into another company. It was now just another theater, and it would remain that way for the next two decades.

The lease became effective at the date of signing and with that, the Constan family ended their connection with the operations of the Avon. However, they continued to own the building until 1989, when it was purchased by the late Bob Lewis. Over the course of the next two decades, though, the Constan family would enjoy a relationship with the Kerasotes chain that has often been described as "unfriendly," to say the least.

The next major renovations at the Avon took place in 1972. It was time, the owners decided, to update the theater's look and bring it into the modern era. Gone were the days of the old-time movie palace and audiences were demanding a slick, modern look for theaters. With that thought in mind, the old fixtures were torn out, the walls were paneled over, new carpet was laid, new seats were installed, and the lobby was given a gaudy, 1970s look that dated the décor in ways that the owners could not have imagined. The addition of the new seats also reduced the capacity of the theater from 900 --what it had been after the Carrier brothers installed the new stage-- to around 700. The old center-door box office was removed and a new one was installed in its current location.

For the next several years, the Avon continued to enjoy success in downtown Decatur, and then in August 1980, the death knell sounded for all the old theaters in town. Some of them were not aware of it yet, but the heyday of Decatur's movie houses was finally coming to an end. It was announced that six movie theaters were being built at the new Hickory Point Mall in nearby Forsyth. The new multiplex was a joint venture of Kerasotes Brothers, which would book the movies, and American Multi-Cinema Inc. of Kansas City, which would operate the business. Placing multiple screens into a single building was a fairly new idea at the time and such theaters were popping up all over America, following closely behind the proliferation of shopping malls.

Business was already beginning to suffer for the downtown theaters. The Lincoln stayed open until December 31, 1980, when it was closed at the end of the Kerasotes lease. The Rogers was closed in 1984, even though its lease actually ran until 1986. It was cheaper, according to the Kerasotes chain, to simply close the place and continue paying the rent than it was to operate it. As for the Avon Theater, said president George Kerasotes, "We have a lease that goes for five and one-half years.

We're obligated by our lease to keep it open. Either keep it open or keep paying the rent."

The theater struggled to stay in business over the next several years, and in 1985, the theater converted to showing second-run movies and changed its name to the Avon Cinema. By this time, the Kerasotes chain had been split apart and George Kerasotes owned the Avon. In April 1986, it turned out that second-run movies just wouldn't pay the bills anymore. The Avon was closed, just a few days after the lease with the Constan family expired. This date would mark the last time that the Avon was part of a theater chain.

Over the course of the next 13 years, the theater alternated between being closed and being home to one failed business plan after another. It operated as a county music opry, a second-run movie theater, and even as a "dollar theater," but nothing worked until 1999 when Skip Huston re-opened the Avon as a full-fledged movie theater again. It has since become one of the largest attractions in downtown Decatur and still operates with three screens today.

And, as mentioned, much of the success of the Avon has been attributed to an otherworldly source.

I have no problem with saying that I believe the Avon Theater to be one of the most haunted places in the city of Decatur. In addition to all the first- and second-hand accounts that I have collected from the place over the years, I have experienced things there myself that have defied all rational attempts to explain them away.

The tales of restless ghosts at the Avon go back to the early 1990s, when I was working on my first book about local ghosts. I advertised widely that I was looking for ghost stories and reportedly haunted spots. The Avon had opened again in 1993 and I was contacted by some of the staff members who worked there. I was able to record a lot of information about the alleged haunting during my visit. The theater manager, and the rest of the staff, reported that things had started to turn up missing in the building, both small items and large. They also told of hearing footsteps in the hallways and offices and felt as if they were being watched.

That night, as I took a walking tour of the place, I found the sensations in some of the areas in the theater were very unsettling. One of the most frightening locations was a hallway that is located upstairs above the theater's lobby. This hallway had been added to the theater during the renovations in 1935 and the theater's offices, and a small bathroom, opened off this corridor. The feeling that I had while walking down this corridor was very disconcerting, and while I certainly don't claim to be psychic, it was a strange experience. I would soon learn that the theater staff felt the same way and largely avoided the place whenever possible. There had been many occasions when the sound of footsteps had echoed in the corridor and those who looked to see who was there found it empty. This corridor would be where more than one person would encounter a ghost.

Unfortunately, the Avon closed again a short time after my visit, and I wondered if I would be able to get inside again. Rumor had it that the theater might be torn down. Later that year, though, I was able to return. Skip Huston, who now operates the theater, was part of a group interested in buying it in 1995. The plan was to turn the place into a movie-themed nightclub that would serve food and drinks, along with films and live entertainment. The project never came about, but I was able to spend quite a bit of time there doing research and prowling about the place. During this brief period, a number of strange encounters took place and several incidents happened that were not easily explained.

I experienced one such incident first-hand. I was in the upstairs hallway one day, taking photographs, and had just passed the first office on the left side of the hall when I felt something take hold of the tail of my shirt. It distinctly felt as though a hand had sharply tugged on it

The Avon Theater as it looked in recent years – literally saved from the wrecking ball more than once.

but --always the skeptic-- I quickly turned around to see if I had somehow snagged it on something or if someone was playing a joke on me. Not only was no one there, but I was nowhere near a door frame or anything else that I could have caught the shirt on. Needless to say, I didn't spend very much more time in the hallway that afternoon.

But of all the things that happened that spring, it has become known for one very bizarre event. It was during this period that Skip came face-to-face with the theater's resident ghost.

During the process of evaluating the building for the nightclub project, Skip came down to the theater one rainy afternoon in the spring of 1995. On this day,

The eerie hallway above the lobby, where so many people have encountered the resident ghost

his trip to the Avon had a double purpose. He was not only looking over the building but was also borrowing some marquee letters for use at an upcoming show at the Lincoln Theater. Even though it was a "dark and stormy" afternoon and he knew the theater was probably haunted, he had no problem with going there by himself. He grabbed a flashlight and a couple of garbage bags to hold the letters and proceeded to the theater.

Skip made his way through the theater to the "letter room," which is located off the previously mentioned hallway on the upstairs level of the building. The room is a small office where all the plastic letters for the theater marquee are stored. After he entered the dimly lit room, he used his flashlight to begin looking for letters and checking them off the sheet he carried with him.

A few minutes after he started working, he distinctly heard a noise behind him in the hallway. He turned around but saw no one there. A few minutes later, he heard it again. Were those footsteps? He looked out into the corridor again, but it was just as dark and empty as it had been before. Skip shook his head and went back to work, hurriedly filling one of the plastic bags with letters. Again, he heard another strange noise and reflexively turned around. This time, he found that he was not alone.

"A man stood in the doorway to the room," Skip recalled. "My first thought was that someone else was in the theater, perhaps a homeless person hiding out there. He was of medium height and slender build. His age appeared to be in his late fifties or early sixties. His hair was close-cropped gray and black. He was not transparent or wraith-like. He appeared solid. His face was nondescript, and he stared into the room, not looking at me, just staring. I started to speak to him and then he slowly turned and started down the hallway. Recovered from my surprise, I darted to the doorway to say something but all that I saw was an empty hall. I grabbed the finished bag of letters and left the theater as fast as my legs would carry me!"

A few years later, the theater finally re-opened. As with any sort of major restoration, a lot of time, money, and hard work was involved. The Avon had deteriorated badly during the time it was closed down and initially it looked as though opening the place would be impossible. There were simply too many things wrong with the old building and every time that one thing got fixed, something else would break down. In addition, Skip had skeptics to deal with among his partners and his staff. They constantly badgered him about the theater's so-called ghosts and poked fun at his belief that the building was haunted. "They started out as skeptics," he laughed later, "but they're all believers now!"

As the restoration and repair work began to shake loose the dust and grime of the building, it awakened other things as well. It was not long before everyone on the crew, including those who had been the most skeptical about the haunting, began to report eerie incidents that they couldn't explain away. Nearly everyone talked of hearing phantom voices in empty rooms and in the deserted auditorium. They also complained of disembodied footsteps and inexplicable cold chills that simply should not exist. Most easily convinced were those who spent the entire night either working or sleeping in the building. They were soon coming to Skip and apologizing for doubting him.

Later, as customers began to arrive at the re-opened theater, they reported their own encounters. Many people spoke of feeling as though they were being watched and of pressure of hands on their backs and arms when no one was present. None of the incidents were particularly frightening. It was more like the resident specter was simply trying to make his presence known.

In the early part of 2005, I was working out of an office at the Avon. One chilly afternoon in March, I was in one of the offices above the lobby, talking to a friend on the telephone. As we were chatting, I happened to glance up and see someone walk past the door of the room, which was open just a few inches. I couldn't see who this person was, or anything about him, just the form of someone walking quickly past.

Assuming that it was another staff member who happened to be in the theater that day, I put down the telephone and got up to speak to him. I left my friend on hold and told her that I would be right back. I quickly opened the door and leaned out to see who was there but saw no movement expect for the door of the room next to the office. It was softly clicking shut and I guessed that whoever it was had gone into the room. I had gotten up too quickly for them to have gone anywhere else and the door that led downstairs to the lobby was shut tight. I walked down the corridor a few steps and opened the door of the next room to say hello. But the room was empty.

I suddenly realized that whoever had been walking down the hallway was not among the living. I hurried back into the office, picked up the telephone again, and told my friend what had happened. She gasped. "What are you going to do?"

I answered that question as I was in the process of doing it. "I'm closing the door to the office," I replied. "That way, if any more ghosts walk by, I won't see them."

After the theater re-opened in 1999, the hauntings at the Avon continued. Weird encounters often occurred with staff members and customers alike, but there was little that was frightening about them.

I believed that each one signaled the continuing presence of Gust Constan, who simply wants us to know that he was still there, watching over the place, hopefully, content with the way that things were going. For the first time in many years, the Avon was a family business again, just like it was in the days of the Constan brothers. It's not hard to imagine that Gust was pleased.

But even our benevolent resident spirit couldn't save the place after Skip passed away in 2025. What will become of the Avon now is anyone's guess. The business is gone forever, but perhaps the building will survive.

CONTRIBUTORS
FOR ISSUE NO. 11

AMANDA R. WOOMER

Writer, anthropologist, and dark historian, Amanda R. Woomer was born and raised in Buffalo, NY. The owner of The Traveling Museum of Memento Mori, she is a featured writer for Haunted Magazine, The Morbid Curious, and the curator of the all-female paranormal journal, The Feminine Macabre. She is the author/co-author of more than 20 books for kids and adults, including *Harlots & Hauntings, The Art of Grieving*, and *Hell Hath No Fury 3* with Troy Taylor. Follow her spooky adventures at spookeats.com and on Facebook, Instagram, and Twitter.

ERIN TAYLOR

Erin Taylor lives in Colorado with her family and fur babies. The paranormal has been one of her passions since she was a small child, and she has been investigating formally since 2013. She recently released her fourth book, Unfinished Business, #2, following behind the first Unfinished Business. Other books include Sleeping Among Spirits and Strange Colorado, Volume 1. All books are self-published and can be found on Amazon. While she's a regular contributor to her favorite cousin's publication, The Morbid Curious, she has also been published in American Paranormal Magazine and Haunted Magazine.

ADAM WHITE

Adam White, a native of a quaint Midwest town, discovered his fascination for the paranormal in his early years after an encounter with a phantom train. This initial spark ignited a lifelong passion that has driven him for over two decades. He has an extensive portfolio of hundreds of cases, articles in magazines and newspapers, and appearances on popular platforms like Coast-to-Coast AM and MTV. Beyond investigations, he has shared his knowledge through teaching workshops and community college courses on the subject. Additionally, for two decades, he has been a dedicated local tour guide for the Haunted Decatur Tours.

SUSAN A. JACOBUCCI

"Sue," Susan A. Jacobucci, hails from Massachusetts, USA. She is an independent researcher and founding associate of K & S Paranormal with her paranormal investigations taking her to haunted locations in the Midwest and Eastern United States. Sue has an upcoming article about the marketability of haunted homes slated for publication in the spring of 2025 in Volume VII of The Feminine Macabre curated by Amanda Woomer and an article about a haunted town hall in Sam Baltrusis's Haunted Travels anthology slated for a June 2025 release. Sue has authored paranormal articles included in Volumes IV and VI of The Feminine Macabre and archaeological pieces that have appeared in American Antiquity, Archaeology of the Northeast, and The Bulletin of the Massachusetts Archaeological Society. Sue earned a Masters in Historical Archaeology, a Bachelor of Science in Anthropology, and a Bachelor of Arts in Sociology.

JAKE BONNETT

Jake Bonnett is a lifelong native of Illinois who grew up in a haunted house, which sparked a lifelong fascination with the macabre and the paranormal. From childhood, he has been deeply interested in death, the afterlife, and the unknown. A cancer survivor, Jake has faced life's fragility firsthand, which has only deepened his curiosity about the darker aspects of human existence. In addition to his personal exploration of the supernatural, Jake is a co-operator and tech specialist of New Age Paranormal, one the oldest active paranormal investigation teams in central Illinois and has taught workshops and college courses on how to perform investigations into the paranormal. He has been part of American Hauntings for many years and has been a guide for the Haunted Decatur Tours for more than a decade.

WENDY HAYWOOD ESKEW

Wendy Haywood Eskew is a lifelong Tennessean who works field of eye care. When not working hard to keep the family cat in the lifestyle he has become accustomed to, she enjoys history and folklore. In her spare time, she loves reading, amateur ghost hunting and all things spooky. It became a lifelong passion while listening to her family's ghost stories and watching horror movies with her father, interests she has now passed on to her own daughter. She was featured in The Morbid Curious #7 and #10.

BARRY COLEMAN

Barry still lives in the same 174-year-old house, with his wife, and part-time entities who have identified themselves as Robert, Frank, Betsy, Ann and someone with the last name Talmage. They all say hello. Coincidentally and unintentionally, they made an offer on the house on Friday the 13th and took possession (pun intended) on October 31.

GINA ARMSTRONG AND VICTORIA VANCEK

Sister team and co-founders of Haunted History BC, Gina Armstrong & Victoria Vancek, blend their passion for the paranormal with a deep interest in history. Residing in the lower mainland ofBritish Columbia, Canada, the spooky sisters began their haunted adventures in 2017. The local authors and historians travel across BC to collaborate with heritage sites, residents, and other paranormal enthusiasts to gather and document stories and evidence. Their unique approach not only entertains but also educates, making them a distinctive presence in the field of paranormal investigation and historical research. In 2021 Gina and Victoria published the first Canadian paranormal magazine, *Evenings & Avenues—Hauntings in the Outskirts*. The sisters continue to co-author the book series which explores ghosts, cryptids, haunted objects, UFO sightings, and local folklore.

In 2023 the sisters took their passion for history and the paranormal and launched local haunted walking tours, a lecture series, and several immersive events. Highlighting their history preservation efforts, their work has been acknowledged through several awards. In December 2024, they were awarded the International Impact Book Award for their book series in the history category. In January of this year, they received the 2025 Canadian Choice Award for their literary contributions.

TROY TAYLOR

Troy Taylor is the author of books on ghosts, hauntings, true crime, the unexplained, and the supernatural in America. He is the founder of American Hauntings Ink, which offers books, ghost tours, events, and the Haunted America Conference, as well as the creator of the American Oddities Museum in Alton, Illinois. He was born and raised in the Midwest and divides his time between Alton, Illinois and wherever the wind decides to take him.

©Colin Batty peculiarium.com

Ludwig Schradler & Sohn

FÜSSEN
Augsburgerstr. 276.

www.ingramcontent.com/pod-product-compliance
Lightning Source LLC
Chambersburg PA
CBHW081642040426
42449CB00015B/3428